e with

elized onions

stewed apricots and fennel with ri... stachios

eet potato–fennel sl... ck peppe

naigrette   sicilian tuna wi... ck olive

chicken salad with walnuts, roasted tomatoes, pickled red onions, and frisée

bacon, lettuce, and

chicken liver pâté with fried onions and radish salad

smoked salmon with avocado green mango, and basil

cheddar with smoked ham, poached pea... and mustard

wich

flatiron steak with cucumber and ginger salad and black chile mayonnaise

goat cheese with avocado, walnut pesto, and watercress

celery, walnut pesto, and

marinated white anchovies with soft-cooked egg, roasted onions, salsa verde, and frisée

salami with marina...

mozzarella and provol... with roast... tomatoes black oliv...

mortadella with radicchio and chio vinaigrette

skirt steak with fried egg, oyster mushrooms, and parsley vinaigrette

'wichcraft

'wichcraft

craft a sandwich into a meal—
and a meal into a sandwich

tom colicchio
WITH sisha ortúzar

TEXT BY **rhona silverbush**

PHOTOGRAPHS BY **bill bettencourt**

Clarkson Potter/Publishers
New York

Copyright © 2009 by TC Enterprises
Photographs copyright © 2009 by Bill Bettencourt

All rights reserved.
Published in the United States by Clarkson Potter/Publishers, an imprint of the
Crown Publishing Group, a division of Random House, Inc., New York.
www.crownpublishing.com
www.clarksonpotter.com

Clarkson Potter is a trademark and Potter with colophon is a registered
trademark of Random House, Inc.

Library of Congress Cataloging-in-Publication Data
Colicchio, Tom.
  'wichcraft: craft a sandwich into a meal—and a meal into a sandwich /
Tom Colicchio with Sisha Ortúzar—1st ed.
  Includes index.
  1. Sandwiches.   2. 'wichcraft (Restaurant)   I. Ortúzar, Sisha.   II. Title.
TX818.C55   2009
641.8'4—dc22   2008027803

978-0-609-61051-0

Printed in China

Design by Amy Sly

10 9 8 7 6 5 4 3 2 1

First Edition

For Lori and Dante
—T.C.

For Jenny
—S.O.

table of contents

'wichmenu
breakfastsandwiches

fried eggs with **bacon, gorgonzola,** and **frisée** 30

onion frittata with **roasted tomato** and **cheddar** 33

skillet egg bruschette 36

pbj 39

kumquat-rosemary marmalade with **goat cheese** 40

smoked ham with **avocado** and **butter** 43

skirt steak with **fried egg, oyster mushrooms,** and **parsley vinaigrette** 44

stewed apricots and **fennel** with **ricotta, pistachios,** and **black pepper** 49

coolsandwiches

goat cheese with **avocado, celery, walnut pesto,** and **watercress** 52

boucheron with **grapefruit** and **crispy olives** 55

egg salad with **caviar** 56

chopped chickpeas with **roasted peppers, black olives, lemon confit,** and **parsley** 59

pan-fried eggplant with **buffalo mozzarella, white anchovies,** and **raisin-pinenut relish** 60

raw yellow beets with **avocado, grapefruit,** and **radish sprouts** 64

smoked salmon with **avocado, green mango,** and **basil** 67

marinated white anchovies with **soft-cooked egg, roasted onions, salsa verde,** and **frisée** 68

continued . . .

sicilian tuna with **fennel, black olives,** and **lemon** 71

lobster with **sweet potato–fennel slaw** and **tarragon vinaigrette** 72

roasted shrimp salad with **tomatoes** and **olives** 75

marinated fresh tuna with **green beans, pickled peppers, garlic,** and **mayonnaise** 76

chicken salad with **walnuts, roasted tomatoes, pickled red onions,** and **frisée** 81

chicken liver pâté with **fried onions** and **radish salad** 82

salami with **marinated cauliflower** and **bitter greens** 85

flatiron steak with **cucumber** and **ginger salad** and **black chile mayonnaise** 86

mortadella with **grilled radicchio** and **pistachio vinaigrette** 89

bacon, lettuce, and **tomato** with **mayonnaise** 91

roast beef with **grilled red onions, radish slaw,** and **black pepper mayonnaise** 92

warmsandwiches

fontina with **black trumpet mushrooms** and **truffle fondue** 96

gruyère with **caramelized onions** 98

roasted asparagus with **red onions, basil,** and **vacherin** 101

cheddar with **smoked ham, poached pear,** and **mustard** 103

mozzarella and **provolone** with **roasted tomatoes** and **black olives** 104

marinated eggplant with **chickpea puree, roasted peppers,** and **watercress** 109

fried squid po-boy with **avocado** and **black chile oil** 110

tuna and **roasted tomato melt** 113

roasted pumpkin with **mozzarella** and **hazelnut brown butter** 114

whipped salt cod with **roasted peppers** and **parsley** 117

fried cod with **tomato salad** and **serrano mayonnaise** 118

chicken breast with **roasted peppers, mozzarella,** and **spinach-basil pesto** 121

roasted turkey with **avocado, bacon, onion marmalade,** and **mayonnaise** 122

pork sausage with **pickled grilled fennel, ricotta,** and **arugula** 125

cured duck breast with **caramelized apples** and **endive** 126

pastrami with **sauerkraut, gruyère,** and **whole-grain mustard sauce** 131

slow-roasted pork with **red cabbage, jalapeños,** and **mustard** 132

continued . . .

roasted pork and **coppa** with **pickled pepper relish** and **fontina** 134

crisp pork belly with **sweet** and **sour endive** 141

grilled sausage with **smoked coleslaw** 151

meatloaf with **cheddar, bacon,** and **tomato relish** 136

roasted pork loin with **prunes, dandelion greens,** and **mustard** 145

beer-braised beef short ribs with **pickled vegetables, aged cheddar,** and **horseradish** 152

red wine–braised flank steak with **roasted peppers, onions,** and **gruyère** 138

roasted leg of lamb with **lemon confit, mustard greens,** and **black olive mayonnaise** 146

sweetsandwiches

chocolate cream'wich 158

peanut butter cream'wich 160

oatmeal cream'wich 162

banana bread with **caramel ice cream** and **pecan brittle** 165

gingerbread with **rum ice cream** and **poached pears** 168

devil's food cake with **vanilla ice cream** and **sour cherries** 171

why a sandwich cookbook?

I've done the math, and as it turns out, about 58 percent of the meals I've eaten in the course of my life have been sandwiches. Breakfast en route to work? Often a sandwich. Lunch without a lunch break? Invariably, a sandwich. And here's a typical dinner, if you happen to be a cook in a restaurant: It's 11 P.M., you had your last snack at about 5 P.M., you've been plating beautiful meals all evening (and no, you're not jaded about them: they smell and look *great*), and you're hungry. You grab two slices of bread, nab the odds-and-ends of the short ribs that were too uneven to be served to patrons, add a slice of cheese, round it out with a swipe of onion relish, and, standing up, enjoy your meal. It's your on-the-fly, catch-as-catch-can, portable meal—a sandwich version of the same entrées your patrons have enjoyed all evening. Such sandwiches not only fed me, they also gave me food for thought.

While working over the years as one of my sous-chefs, Sisha Ortúzar has become a trusted emissary, someone who understands my way of doing things so well that I bring him with me to open new restaurants in other cities. Turns out Sisha had given the humble sandwich a lot of thought himself, and he wanted to open a sandwich shop. We talked about it, and I could see his ideas dovetailed with my own: namely, that a sandwich should be a portable meal sourced and crafted with the same intention and excitement as we brought to the food in our restaurants. From day one, the idea was to create "Craft between two pieces of bread."

What did that mean exactly? I used the day-after Thanksgiving sandwich as my guide. Ask yourself: why is a sandwich made from Thanksgiving leftovers so good? Because everything in it was originally crafted for a great meal. The turkey is roasted for the table, with all the flavor and juiciness that implies, the mashed potatoes are creamy and satisfying. The gravy, the cranberries—it's all made from real food, and nothing is "filler." It all adds up to a robust and balanced plate that is even better the next day, between two slices of bread.

That became our mission: to seek out the same quality, artisanal ingredients as we use at Craft; to put real thought into a menu of sandwiches, any one of which would work just as well deconstructed backward into a meal; and to give people fine food without the demands of a reservation or a long time commitment. In creating the sandwiches we used a musical analogy: a great band, no matter how talented the individual musicians, must work harmoniously together to develop a memorable sound. Since every element of a sandwich gets delivered all at once, no one flavor could overwhelm the rest. Texture is important because the sandwiches need to hold together in one hand. The bread has to be fresh and distinctive. And while everyone likes good value, we opted out of the classic American two-pounds-o'-meat colossus model; portability is paramount, and no one can—or should—eat that much, never mind on the run.

Sisha and I spent a lot of time tossing ideas back and forth. We ate a lot of sandwiches. We emerged with about two dozen that satisfied our aims for balance and flavor. We opened the doors in a space two doors down from Craft during the summer of 2003.

And that first store taught us some crucial lessons. First, never open in the summer without air-conditioning! Second, listen to your customers.

From day one, New Yorkers showed up and made their thoughts known, in person and via e-mail. We took notes. Jeffrey Zurofsky joined our team and helped us grow. We created a central commissary where we could slow-roast Berkshire pork, hand-pull mozzarella, and churn homemade ice cream for all of the stores. We found it was possible to make "fast" food from green-market vegetables and antibiotic- and hormone-free meat. We obtained ingredients from small producers and artisan farmers. We formed a partnership with the Fresh Air Fund to train and employ inner-city kids, whose energy and creativity we enjoyed. With the help of numerous talented and committed individuals, today 'wichcraft has expanded to a dozen New York City locations and outposts in San Francisco and Las Vegas. I'm happy to say that our customers are still checking in regularly, letting us know when we get it right (and wrong). In truth, we owe our success to them.

And by extension, they've helped us hone the thoughts and recipes in this book—ways not only to conceptualize sandwiches from meals but, if you wish, also to craft meals from the sandwich recipes contained herein. So, to answer my initial question, that's "why a sandwich cookbook."

Cook often, eat well.

TOM COLICCHIO

more than chewing the fat

TOM & SISHA on the salad days
of their sandwich shops

Q *How did 'wichcraft come about?*

TOM Well, it actually goes back to before the opening of Craftbar . . .

SISHA Wait, Craftbar? It does?

TOM Yeah, because we were kicking around ideas for the name of the new restaurant, and my wife, Lori, threw out "'wichcraft," and we all thought it was really clever, but it doesn't tell the whole story of that restaurant, so we scrapped it and ended up choosing the name Craftbar. Soon the space that was next door to Craftbar became available, and we were all in my office one day thinking about what we could do there, and we thought about doing a raw bar; we considered a few other things and, Sisha, you said, "Listen, we already have this great name, 'wichcraft—let's do sandwiches." And at the time, Sisha was kind of known for making these great sandwiches.

SISHA Thanks. But my recollection is slightly different, because I don't recall knowing about the name. The way I remember it, we were in South Carolina, doing a wine dinner at Kiawah . . .

TOM OK . . .

SISHA And after the dinner we went to get something to eat and we drove into town and went to Melvin's.

TOM Oh, right, yeah.

SISHA We went to get a burger . . .

TOM The barbecue joint, yeah.

SISHA Yeah, but I went for the burgers. They're great.

TOM They are.

SISHA And I remember they were closing, but the kid let us in, so we were talking, and you were thinking about the space and the idea of, like, doing a raw bar or Craftbar-to-go type of thing, and then I brought this idea I'd been having of wanting to do sandwiches, and then you said, "All right, sure, let's do that." And I thought, "Really? Just like that? Wow, that was easy." And then, on the car ride back to the hotel, I said, "So, really, you want to do this?" And you just said, "Sure, let's do it." And then, back in New York—that's when we were all at that meeting and you said, "I have the name." And, of course, "'wichcraft" was just perfect!

TOM Well, you know, you were already making these great sandwiches for everybody.

SISHA Oh, you mean in Vegas.

Q *Why were you making sandwiches in Vegas?*

SISHA In a traditional restaurant you do "family meal," where you cook for the staff. Down at Craftsteak in Vegas, at the end of the night I would grab some scraps, steak scraps, or whatever was around, and

make sandwiches for the staff, and people were excited about them, which just kind of got me started thinking.

TOM All cooks do that, at the end of the night. If they're hungry, they grab little ends of whatever they have around, grab some vegetables, put them between two pieces of bread, and stand up and eat it.

SISHA Exactly, so we figured, why not do that type of food as sandwiches generally, since you don't typically see that happening in a sandwich shop.

TOM And at this point Sisha had been working with me for, what, seven years about?

SISHA Yeah, something like that.

TOM So, it wasn't like somebody coming out of the blue whom you'd have to indoctrinate to understand Craft style, so—

SISHA I'd been doing Tom's food for a couple of years and had come to really understand it from the core—to understand the philosophy—and Tom could just say to me or to other chefs who'd been working with him for a while, "do this," and we'd all just know what he's talking about.

TOM We talked a little bit about this in the first book, *Think Like a Chef.* You develop a language, so if someone says, "Take the sole, braise it in beurre fondue, and add blanched asparagus," we all know exactly what we're talking about. We know, number one, that the fish is going to be impeccably fresh, we know how to make the beurre fondue, we know what braising in that beurre fondue means, and we know just how the asparagus needs to be blanched.

SISHA We understand it.

TOM And I knew that undertaking a new enterprise like 'wichcraft was going to be so much easier to do with someone coming from within: I wouldn't have to

micromanage at this point because I knew what I was going to get. And in general, as regards the chefs who are running the various restaurants, I let them do what they know how to do. Once the restaurants are up and running, I have occasional tweaks, but I'm never, ever concerned that I'm going to walk into a restaurant and see anything egregious.

SISHA Yeah, coming up in the restaurants ensures that there's definitely a common language.

TOM So at the first menu conversation, I don't remember where it was, I just recall throwing ideas out there.

SISHA Yeah, and then I wrote a menu, and gave it to you and you liked it, so we actually started making the sandwiches at Craftbar to test them out. And before we opened, we started making a few and selling them as a special at Craftbar for lunch, to get some feedback from patrons and the staff.

Q *And how long a process was that?*

TOM Not long.

SISHA A couple of months, while we were doing the construction of the space.

Q *And what are your recollections of the process of designing the shop, the space itself, to complement what you were trying to do with the food?*

TOM We had no idea what we were doing.

SISHA None.

TOM In fact, we're still in the process of discovering all the levels on which 'wichcraft is a very different business from Craft. I mean, even with basic decisions about the flow through the space, such as where and how to set the cash registers, the considerations are altogether different from these at the other Craft restaurants, plus we didn't start having a commissary, as we do now, so it was very different: everything was being prepped and cooked there, some things were being prepped at Craft, so we had a lot of stuff to work out.

SISHA Right. The space that became our first 'wichcraft was a short-term lease, so we knew that whatever we were doing there would be only for a short time. So we decided that we would spend as little money as possible designing the space, because the endeavor was less about designing a restaurant and more about testing an idea. And, I mean, we did make some poor decisions, such as believing that we could keep the air conditioner from the old store and, you know, the summer hit and it was hot.

TOM It was so hot.

SISHA We got a review from the *New York Times* and three-quarters of it talked about how hot it was! But we learned.

TOM That's how the third wheel came about.

SISHA Right.

Q *The third wheel?*

TOM Jeffrey Zurofsky, our managing partner. I had met Jeffrey years before when Gramercy Tavern was opening. Right after opening 'wichcraft, Jeffrey called me up and reintroduced himself, and he asked to meet with me. He walked into the office and put a document on my desk. And I said, what's this? He said, well, it's a business plan for a sandwich place I'd wanted to do, but you beat me to it, so I want to come work with you. And my response was, "I usually don't take people from the outside, so you'd have to come in and work for a minimum of three months, and, quite frankly, it's Sisha's decision as to whether or not you stay on." Once he got through

that period, and it was clear that it was going to work out, then we really started thinking more about growing and doing more.

SISHA That's when we came up with the concept of having the commissary kitchen, because we realized that the concept of what we do is so reliant on actual cooking, as opposed to slicing meats and bread. So if we were going to operate more than one 'wichcraft, they needed to be consistent: the offerings needed to be the same and to be great all the time.

TOM If we didn't create a central commissary, we would have been forced to hire chefs for every location. And if we were going to cook in each location, then we also would have had to find spaces that are bigger, which would have limited us to spaces that you can duct, that can accept gas appliances.

SISHA So we started working on the second location and the commissary while still working out of the original little store. And then, actually, the second location opened before the commissary, so we rented a kitchen for a few months.

TOM 'wichcraft is definitely moving ahead, but, you know, right now it doesn't even feel like a restaurant. I mean, it feels more like a tech start-up. We have a bunch of young men and women working hard, playing hard, and there's great energy—you feel like you're really doing something. A restaurant is so different from this, because when you open a restaurant, it is pulled together, opening night comes, and then you maintain it. 'wichcraft, on the other hand, always feels like it keeps moving with this forward thrust. The great thing about this organization is that I'm never met with a "We can't do that" attitude just because we're a small company; rather, the approach is always "All right, let's find a way to do it!"

SISHA Here's an example: One of our guys is currently hard at work trying to figure out how we're going to

implement "the daily roast." It's an idea that Tom has had for a long time.

TOM One thing I've always loved—again, from the experience cooks have of making their sandwiches while on the line—is this: there's a roast of something, and you're slicing, and you soak the bread in all the juices that are coming off the meat, add some of the meat itself, and that's it—that's basically the whole sandwich. Maybe you're drizzling on some olive oil or adding some arugula—and that's the sandwich. So I would like to have a roast of the day in each store, where there's someone actually carving it and putting it on a sandwich, and that's it. I put the idea out to the others, and their response was "Well, let's go ahead!"

SISHA The reason we haven't to date is . . .

TOM It's hard to pull off well.

SISHA Not because it's hard to do, but because it's easy to have it not look good.

TOM Right.

SISHA It's easy to do poorly. We've all experienced a roast that's sat a little bit too long in the heat, and it's dry and just not good. And we'd have to implement this without a chef and a kitchen in each store while continuing our current service.

TOM Delivery is another example of something that's easy to do poorly. We started small and let the delivery business grow . . .

SISHA What is it now, twenty percent of our business, Tom?

TOM About that, yeah. We do three hundred deliveries a day. It's the type of thing, though, that's very easy to do a bad job at; it's very easy to screw up. And we screw up every once in a while. Every day there's, you know, one or two problems: we forgot a soup, we forgot this or that. But there are days when we pull it off without a single hangup, and an e-mail goes around to everyone saying "Congratulations, what a great job." And it's an inspiration to everyone, 'cause it's one of those things that you can do very poorly very easily. That business has grown tremendously. And I credit our people's can-do attitude; they chose to believe that we'd figure it out and make it work. And that, I think, is why we're doing so well. There's always the attitude that if it's a good idea, and it's passed muster, then the question is only how we do it, how we figure it out.

Q *When you think back to being at Melvin's and remember what you thought you might do, and then you look around at what you actually have created . . .*

SISHA There wasn't this huge plan back then.

TOM Yeah, I mean, we never sat down with pad and paper and said, "OK, we're going to grow this into thirty outlets in five years."

SISHA We were only thinking, "Let's just make sandwiches in this temporary rental space next door."

TOM Exactly, and see what happens with it. Though in the back of our minds I think we also knew that, for this to be successful, we would have to do multiple stores because there's only so much you can do at one small store, doing sandwiches. So we always thought, "Well, you know, if we do it right, there's probably a good opportunity to do a couple more in the city." But that's all we thought. We certainly

didn't realize how many we could do and how far a net we could cast.

Q *On a substantive level, it seems that what you're doing now really is the outgrowth, or child, of Craft.*

TOM Yes, it fits into the whole expansion model of Craft, similar to that of clothing designers, where we're hitting different price points with different products, all comporting with a single vision and mission. And so, from Craft's standpoint, it fits into that. Craft and Craftsteak, then Craftbar, then 'wichcraft all hit different price points and open us up to all types of diners and markets.

SISHA We have a joke about getting even further into the market with "Tacolicchio," the taco stand.

Q *Meanwhile, back at 'wichcraft, where do you find yourselves right now?*

TOM We can make a sandwich really well right now, we can run a commissary, we can obtain ingredients—all those things that we know how to do. The big question now is, can we continue to run and grow in a multi-unit concept.

Q *What's your greatest challenge?*

TOM I'd say the hardest challenge we have is how to ensure that we continue to do things in the way we believe, from obtaining quality ingredients down to the smallest details. If you have one store and you train its two chefs to be consistent in how much mayonnaise is used in a particular sandwich, for example, that's easy. But how do you do that in multiple places and make sure the sandwiches look the same at all of the locations, given that it's not frozen or in a squeeze bottle? These kind of things.

SISHA If you look at many fast-food places, for example, there's nothing left to chance.

TOM Whereas because of what we're doing, there's a lot left to chance. You do rely on people, but everybody wants to build a better mousetrap, and stuff starts to change. And you don't even realize it, because it happens in such a small, incremental way. Then all of a sudden, before you know it, you're wondering how this or that happened.

SISHA And in ten different places, in ten different ways.

TOM Yeah.

Q *And if 'wichcrafts wind up in different cities, or even different countries . . .*

TOM There would be a regional manager responsible to preserve the integrity. That's the hard part about growing: finding people who are as committed to our philosophy and practices as we are. I mean, many people who invest in or run chains would be shocked to find out that we buy from small suppliers. And why aren't we buying cheap products?

SISHA That's what many food service operations do: one-stop shopping, a single truck pulls up that provides everything from one company.

TOM Most people would look at us and say, "You know what? You can probably still sell that cheese sandwich, but you can buy a lot cheaper stuff to put in it."

SISHA And great, but that's not what we do. Our tomatoes, for example, are delivered in the summer by the farmer on his way to the greenmarket. At six in the morning he stops by our store and drops off the tomatoes. We get our sauerkraut from a guy in the market who sends us a bucket of it in the mail; that's how he works, and we've had to adapt to that because we want that guy's sauerkraut. A lot of people might wonder, "Why

would you make it so hard on yourself?" Or, "Why do you make this pantry item from scratch, when you can just buy it already made?" But that's just what we do. We cook. We buy food, not a commodity.

TOM That's our DNA. You have to keep that DNA as you grow; you can't forget it. We have to run this business almost as if we had one store, and it's next door to the mother ship, and that's it. If we maintain that attitude, then we'll find a way to keep it in practice, and we'll be fine.

Q *This seems very forward thinking, since we're coming to learn that the modifications to farming practices and to the food itself might have been cost-effective for agribusiness, but it's bad for consumers and the planet. You seem to embrace a return to an earlier way of raising and creating what we eat.*

TOM A big part of our philosophy involves working with smaller farmers who are growing multiple crops and raising animals on the same farm. These farmers don't need to fertilize their soil to death, for example, which is highly problematic for the ecosystem and, ultimately, for the consumer of the product. Of course, buying from small farmers is more expensive.

SISHA People have come to expect that meat should be cheap: they've gotten used to chicken and beef being dirt cheap, but it shouldn't be . . . which is actually OK, because people also shouldn't be eating so much of it. We simply shouldn't be eating meat three times a day as we do.

TOM We're excited to think that 'wichcraft is part of a movement taking people in the direction that they themselves should want to go in, and that they then can translate that understanding into what they choose to do with this cookbook in their own homes. Everything we're discussing today and in the cookbook is a philosophy

behind approaching buying and cooking. With 'wichcraft and this cookbook, the meals we are creating just happen to be portable. At the end of the day, we're looking to grow a business with a great product and great food that is supplied by people who are growing food responsibly. And then we're also looking to provide a great atmosphere for the employees. You know, if we can do that . . .

SISHA When Jeffrey and I talk and he asks me, "What's your motivation?" I realize that, above all else, I want to be really happy and proud about what we do, in large part because of what we're creating and how we're operating in the world while we do so, and also because our patrons like coming here, and because people are happy to work here.

Q *In applying the principles that govern 'wichcraft to making sandwiches in one's own home, what would you advise your readers?*

SISHA Don't get caught up in trends instead of doing what you happen to like. And, of course, use good food.

TOM Yes, please think about the quality of your ingredients and where they're coming from. And then, don't be afraid to try things, to experiment. Some people get so bogged down in what goes together, what's "right" with what. Let go of that and just play with what seems interesting or pleasing to you—what you like. That's what we do, and it works, and it will work for you. Just use a little common sense and jump right in, and don't be afraid to do stuff. And enjoy the process.

breakfast sandwiches

fried eggs with bacon, gorgonzola, and frisée

8 thick slices bacon

4 ciabatta rolls

4 tablespoons gorgonzola dolce or other mild blue cheese

2 cups frisée lettuce

1 teaspoon extra-virgin olive oil

1 teaspoon red wine vinegar

Kosher salt and freshly ground black pepper

2 tablespoons unsalted butter

8 large eggs, preferably pasture-raised

Most of us have had the classic egg-and-bacon sandwich. When conceiving of our own, we were inspired by the French salad of *frisée au lardons,* in which the bacon lardons are rendered and warmed up, gorgonzola is used for the dressing, and the frisée is tossed into the mix, becoming warm and wilted. Here, we have essentially married the salad and the classic sandwich, and the resulting 'wich illustrates that, by just doing a little more, you can take a standard sandwich to a higher realm.

If you are preparing this recipe for a large number of people, you can fry the eggs and set them aside on parchment paper on a tray, popping them in the oven to heat them just a bit when you're ready to assemble the sandwiches. This sandwich would be great made with poached eggs, as well. **MAKES 4 SANDWICHES**

Preheat the oven to 350°F.

In a heavy ovenproof skillet over medium-high heat, cook the bacon until golden brown and crisp on both sides. Transfer to paper towels to drain. Slice the ciabatta rolls in half. Evenly spread 1 tablespoon of the gorgonzola on each bottom slice of bread and place all the bread slices into the oven. While the bread is toasting, toss the frisée in the oil and vinegar, and add salt and pepper to taste.

In a medium-hot skillet, melt the butter and fry the eggs, two to four at a time (depending on the size of your skillet). Flip the eggs halfway through and cook until the yolks are solid around the edges and oozy in the middle. Season the eggs with salt and pepper. Once the bread is toasted and the cheese has melted, remove the bread from the oven. Place the eggs on top of the gorgonzola, followed by the bacon, and finally the dressed frisée. Close the sandwiches and serve.

onion frittata with roasted tomato and cheddar

The Italian version of an omelet, in which the whisked eggs and the other ingredients go into a large pan at the same time, a frittata can be eaten warm or cold. Almost any kind of vegetable works well in a frittata. We love the sweetness and flavor of leeks and roasted onions. The original sandwich at 'wichcraft contained only the frittata and good, aged Cheddar cheese. Ben Bohen, a long-time collaborator, would have this sandwich as his regular breakfast—except that Ben would always add roasted tomato. He encouraged the staff to try it, and he encouraged the customers to try it, until eventually he converted us all and we put it on the menu forevermore with Ben's roasted tomatoes. **MAKES 4 SANDWICHES**

Preheat the oven to 300°F.

In a 10-inch ovenproof skillet, heat the oil and sauté the leek over low heat until soft but without color. In a large bowl, crack and whip the eggs and add the cream, Parmesan cheese, salt, pepper, and oregano. Add the leek and the onions. Pour the egg mixture back into the skillet and place in the oven. Bake the frittata for about 30 minutes, until the center is set. Use immediately or allow to cool (keeps in fridge for about 1 day).

Increase the oven to 350°F or preheat if preparation has been delayed.

Slice the ciabatta rolls in half and place one slice of Cheddar on each top and bottom slice of bread. Place the bread in the oven and remove once cheese is melted. Simultaneously, reheat the frittata in oven if made ahead of time.

Cut the frittata into four pieces and place one piece on each bottom slice of bread. Top with the roasted tomatoes. Close the sandwiches and serve.

1 tablespoon extra-virgin olive oil

1 cup diced leek (white part only)

6 large eggs, preferably pasture-raised

½ cup heavy cream

2 tablespoons grated Parmesan cheese

2 teaspoons kosher salt

½ teaspoon finely ground black pepper

2 teaspoons chopped fresh oregano, or 1 teaspoon dried Sicilian oregano

½ cup Roasted Onions (page 182)

4 ciabatta rolls

8 slices white Cheddar cheese

8 tablespoons Roasted Tomatoes (see page 195)

sandwich architecture

An essay on architecture in a sandwich cook-book? Well, people commonly speak of "building a sandwich," and when we construct one, we do pay attention to its structure and design, usually without realizing it. The issue is worth thinking about when embarking on some serious sandwich making, as we hope you're about to do.

We first gave the matter of sandwich architecture some thought when we were considering the architecture and design of the space that would become our first 'wichcraft location, on East 19th Street in New York City. In working with our architect, we learned a lot about building materials and how they would affect the store. We learned to assess the relationships among aesthetics, functionality, and durability—sometimes the hard way. For example, we loved the spareness of the store's design and were excited to carry that theme throughout the design components, including the wooden floor, which we decided to paint white. (You see where we're heading.)

Oh, it was going to be so beautiful, so starkly beautiful, so vivid and arresting. And it was—the day before we opened. But within five minutes of our grand opening, we were horrified to see black scuff marks and city-street muck transferred to our floors from the bottoms of shoes. It was horrible. The floors looked extra dirty because they were white; there was no keeping them clean. (And in case you're wondering, black scuff marks don't come off a white floor.) Lesson learned: if white floors were so important we would have to paint them once a week (they weren't, and we didn't). Similarly, if you badly want a sandwich that will taste a particular way, but will be so sloppy and juicy that you can eat it only in private, hunched over your kitchen sink, that's OK, too. But if you're making canapés for a cocktail party, and people will eat them while holding a glass of wine in their other hand, the canapés must be constructed differently. Just as we needed to balance aesthetics, functionality, and durability in building and designing our stores, we needed to consider the interplay of similar elements in sandwich construction as well.

With sandwiches, *aesthetics* refers not only to the visual but also to the taste and texture, as well as to the less tangible and more highly subjective "Wow" factor (the excitement value that a marriage of favorite ingredients will elicit). Regarding *durability,* you must ask when the sandwich is to be eaten, for example. Is it for the upcoming meal? For a three-hour flight later in the day? For a party the following day? It's also important to consider how the ingredients will interact with each other over time (texture plays a role here as well). In our stores, we can build some of the panini the night before; some sandwich ingredients are made in advance while others must be made on the spot.

For *functionality,* we ask who will eat the sandwich and under what circumstances. Is it for a small child? Thick bread slices or too many ingredients may not fit into a little mouth. For corporate executives at a meeting? Soundness of construction can prevent that dollop of mayo from hitting the boss's silk tie. And it isn't enough to consider each of these elements on its own: by juxtaposing them and weighing their relative importance, you can best achieve your goals each time.

Sandwich architecture necessarily begins and ends with the bread. While we discuss bread more generally elsewhere (see page 46), here are a few words that pertain directly to sandwich architecture. First, the bread must hold up to the task of keeping the sandwich intact, yet the texture of the sandwich should derive from the ingredients within as opposed to from the bread itself. How often have you bit into a sandwich with very coarse or crunchy bread, only to have all of the ingredients spill out the sides? Of course, if the contents are very wet, as with a tuna sandwich, a somewhat crustier bread may well make sense because the bread must have enough texture to withstand the moisture. But generally you want the ingredients to establish the overall texture.

Second, when a 'wichcraft sandwich recipe calls for toasting the bread, toast it on one side only and place the toasted side on the inside of the sandwich. We do this for a few reasons: (1) the bread can absorb moisture from the ingredients and still retain its structure; (2) the toasted side creates a barrier that keeps the softer side from getting soggy; and (3) with the softer side out, you can enjoy the toasted bread without scratching your upper palate. We were pleasantly surprised to find that customers notice and appreciate this small detail.

Third, sometimes we use a roll and cut the bottom thicker than the top, as with our Salami with Marinated Cauliflower and Bitter Greens sandwich (page 85), in which we then heap the marinated cauliflower on the bread. The cauliflower is wonderfully juicy and oily, which makes the bread delicious, but because the bread is cut thicker on the bottom and has a slight crust to it, it retains the moisture—and the flavor!—and the cauliflower does not spill out while you eat it.

Fourth, because every bite will be the same in a sandwich, there must be a balance of ingredients to ensure a good experience throughout. That's why composition really counts! For example, we're very strict about how our bacon, lettuce, and tomato sandwich is built. We don't want the lettuce next to the tomato (and, as a general rule, we never want lettuce near a liquid such as oil, as the oil will pool in the lettuce, making a mess and not distributing to the rest of the sandwich). Mayo blends beautifully with tomato but not with lettuce. Therefore, a BLT should be assembled in the following order: mayonnaise, tomato, bacon, and then lettuce. Even though the ingredients will mix in the mouth, the way they feel and taste when you bite into the sandwich is important. Architecture helps ensure an optimal experience in that regard as well.

A few more tips:

- Keep mustard and mayo apart from one another in a sandwich (if they appear together at all!). Otherwise, the mayo will dilute the flavor of the mustard, making it seem of poorer quality.
- Place cheese in a sandwich near the bread. It further reinforces the structure and durability of the sandwich. But if the cheese is melted with meat, place it next to the meat instead, to add richness and dimension.
- Dress greens before placing them in the sandwich; this ensures that every bite is properly seasoned.

The methods here are not the sole domain of delis, diners, and restaurants. While you may not have given the matter much thought, you've likely applied your own rules of sandwich making since childhood. By pointing out the interplay of aesthetics, functionality, and durability, we simply offer a framework for what you've been doing on your own.

skillet egg bruschette

1 tablespoon extra-virgin olive oil

1 cup diced potato, skin on

¼ teaspoon red pepper flakes

1 cup diced zucchini

Kosher salt and freshly ground black pepper

¼ cup diced pecorino cheese

1 tablespoon chopped fresh oregano, or ½ tablespoon dried Sicilian oregano

½ cup diced smoked ham or bacon lardons

1 tablespoon unsalted butter

1 tablespoon minced garlic

12 cremini or white button mushrooms, cleaned and cut into quarters

¼ cup white wine

2 tablespoons roughly chopped flat-leaf parsley

¼ cup diced fontina cheese

8 large eggs, preferably pasture-raised

8 slices country bread

This open-faced sandwich is similar in many ways to a Spanish tortilla. It's best made in really well-seasoned cast-iron skillets that were passed down from your grandmother. And there's a great side benefit: the dish is perfect for brunch guests, since it looks so good (and thus makes *you* look so good) when you're serving it! **MAKES 8 BRUSCHETTE (2 PER PERSON)**

Preheat the oven to 350°F.

Pour the oil into a small ovenproof cast-iron skillet over medium-high heat. Add the potato and red pepper flakes and cook until the potato is fork-tender. Add the zucchini, season with salt and pepper, and continue cooking until the zucchini is soft, about 3 minutes. Add the pecorino and oregano, and gently toss to mix.

In another small, hot ovenproof skillet, add the ham and butter, and sauté until the ham is slightly crisp. Transfer the ham to paper towels to drain and discard half the butter from the skillet. Add the garlic and mushrooms, season with salt and pepper, and sauté until the mushrooms are dark brown in color, about 5 minutes. Add the wine and stir to scrape up bits from the pan. Add the ham, parsley, and fontina and toss to mix.

Crack four eggs into each skillet, covering the whole skillet with the eggs, and cook over medium heat. Season the eggs with salt and pepper and, once the eggs start to set, transfer both skillets to the oven. Cook for about 5 minutes, until the eggs are soft but not runny.

Meanwhile, grill the bread on both sides. Once the eggs are cooked, remove and cut each skillet of eggs into four pieces. Top each slice of bread with one piece of the skillet eggs. Serve one slice of each per person.

pbj

At 'wichcraft, we make our own peanut butter and we make our own jelly, usually strawberry, Concord grape, and for a brief time in the spring, rhubarb. We feel that even the humble peanut butter and jelly sandwich deserves the finest ingredients. Here's one of our top secrets: we doctor up standard peanut butter by adding real butter, which mellows the flavor, adds richness, and makes the texture more velvety. Is it excessive or—as some have suggested—even evil to add butter to peanut butter? Well, we think of it as substituting one fat for another, modest as long as you spread the same amount on your sandwich. **MAKES 4 SANDWICHES**

4 cups diced trimmed rhubarb

2 cups plus 1 teaspoon sugar

Juice from 1 lemon

1 teaspoon powdered pectin

8 tablespoons peanut butter

8 slices Pullman bread

TO MAKE THE RHUBARB JELLY, in a bowl, combine the rhubarb, 2 cups sugar, and lemon juice and refrigerate overnight in a tightly covered container. The next day, in a small saucepan, bring the rhubarb-and-sugar mixture to a boil. Reduce the heat and simmer for about 5 minutes. Remove from the heat and set aside.

In a small bowl, combine the pectin and remaining teaspoon sugar and temper it by adding small amounts of the hot rhubarb mixture and quickly stirring it. Add it to the rest of the rhubarb and return the saucepan to the stove and bring to a boil. Remove from the heat and place into a clean container with a lid. Once it has cooled down, close the lid and store in the refrigerator for up to 2 weeks.

TO MAKE THE SANDWICHES, evenly spread the peanut butter on 4 slices of bread. Spread 2 tablespoons of jelly on each of the other 4 slices. Close the sandwiches, cut into halves, and serve.

kumquat-rosemary marmalade with goat cheese

¼ cup water

¼ cup sugar

12 ounces kumquats
(about 25 pieces), rinsed,
cut into ¼-inch rounds, and
seeds removed

½ teaspoon black peppercorns,
coarsely crushed

¼ teaspoon finely chopped
fresh rosemary,
plus 1 small sprig

4 slices multigrain bread

6 tablespoons soft goat
cheese (chèvre)

This is a spin on the cream cheese and jam sandwich. We thought the tartness of the goat cheese would marry well with the sweetness of the marmalade, with the rosemary accent to wake you up in the gentlest, nicest of ways and the multigrain bread sending you off on your day feeling you've eaten a meal. The marmalade could certainly be made with oranges or grapefruit—the rosemary would complement them as well. **MAKES 4 OPEN-FACED SANDWICHES**

In a saucepan over medium-low heat, combine the water and sugar and stir occasionally until the sugar has dissolved. Add the kumquats, peppercorns, and fresh rosemary sprig. Stir to mix, making sure to bury the rosemary in the kumquats. Bring to a simmer and cook for 10 to 15 minutes, until the kumquats are translucent and the liquid has reduced to the consistency of a thin syrup. Remove from the heat and discard the sprig of rosemary and any needles that may have separated. Add the chopped rosemary and set aside to cool. Once cold, transfer to a container.

Lightly toast the bread. Evenly spread the goat cheese on each slice of bread and top with a generous amount of the kumquat marmalade. Cut each slice in half (if desired) and serve. (Any leftover marmalade keeps well in the refrigerator for several weeks.)

smoked ham with avocado and butter

Growing up in Chile, Sisha often ate a breakfast of avocado on toast, adding olive oil, salt, pepper, and sometimes ham. So this simple sandwich evolved, like many breakfast foods, into an excellent snack. Please note that with a simple recipe such as this, it is all the more critical that each ingredient be top-notch. Of course, the obvious place to start is with quality smoked ham. But don't forget, too, that a perfectly ripe avocado will add the best texture and flavor and that a fresh bakery baguette will have that incomparable French bread taste. As for the butter? Unsalted gives you control over how much and what kind of salt to add. And your sandwich will reach a higher level altogether if made with fresh butter from a local farm. **MAKES 3 TO 4 SANDWICHES**

1 ripe avocado, halved, pitted, peeled, and sliced

Extra-virgin olive oil

Kosher salt and freshly ground black pepper

2 tablespoons unsalted butter, softened

1 baguette, split lengthwise

8 ounces smoked ham, in thick slices

NOTE This sandwich would also work well as a pressed sandwich.

On a plate, season the avocado with a drizzle of oil and salt and pepper to taste. Spread the butter on the bottom slice of the baguette, and top with the avocado and the ham. Close the sandwich, slice into three or four pieces, and serve.

skirt steak with fried egg, oyster mushrooms, and parsley vinaigrette

2 tablespoons extra-virgin olive oil

1 teaspoon minced garlic

8 ounces oyster mushrooms, sliced in half

Kosher salt and freshly ground black pepper

2 tablespoons Parsley Vinaigrette (page 180)

1 pound skirt steak

2 tablespoons unsalted butter

4 large eggs, preferably pasture-raised

4 ciabatta rolls

We created this for the opening of our Las Vegas store, knowing that it would be the perfect sandwich to have after a night of Vegas-style fun. The richness of both the steak and the eggs is balanced by the acidity and savoriness of the vinaigrette used to season the mushrooms. **MAKES 4 SANDWICHES**

Add the oil to a medium skillet over medium-high heat. Add the garlic, and once the garlic is fragrant, add the mushrooms and season with salt and pepper. Continue cooking until the mushrooms are soft and golden in color, about 5 minutes. Remove from the heat and transfer the mushrooms to a bowl. Add the vinaigrette and toss to coat. Set aside.

Season the meat with salt and pepper and place in a cast-iron skillet over medium-high heat. Cook the meat for 3 to 4 minutes on each side, until browned all over. Remove from the heat and transfer the meat to the bowl with the mushrooms, resting the meat on top to allow the juices to drip onto the mushrooms. Keep in a warm place until ready to use.

In a medium-hot skillet, heat the butter and fry the eggs, two to four at a time, depending on the size of your skillet. Flip the eggs halfway through and cook until the yolk is solid around the edges and oozy in the middle. Season the eggs with salt and pepper.

Thinly slice the meat against the grain. Cut the ciabatta rolls in half and scoop out some of the bread from the top halves. Place slices of the meat on each bottom half and top with the mushrooms, followed by the eggs. Close the sandwiches, cut into halves, and serve.

bread basics

While bread is inarguably the defining ingredient in a sandwich, it is not the star of the show. Yes, its role in keeping the sandwich together is major, but it is literally a supporting role; the bread should be gracious enough to take second billing to the inner ingredients. When the taste of the bread is too prominent (as with many sourdoughs that would be lovely on their own but overpowering in a sandwich), or the texture is too harsh, the sandwich is doomed. So when conceptualizing a sandwich, think from the inside out and let the filling ingredients dictate the choice of bread, based not only on what will best enhance their flavors but also what will work technically and practically.

This is not to say that sometimes fillings don't benefit from an interesting bread that will serve as an ingredient in its own right. For example, if you're making a chicken salad, a semolina bread with raisins would probably add a lot (and, in fact, people often add grapes to their chicken salad—same idea). A nut bread would work well in that instance, too. On the other hand, if you're crafting a sandwich with prosciutto and taleggio cheese, do you really want nuts with that? Similarly, would you put olives on your peanut butter and jelly sandwich? Well, then, don't reach for the olive bread, either. If you do choose a bread with fruit, nuts, seeds, olives, or onions, remember that if you then heat the bread, whether by toasting it or putting it on the grill or in a pan, you are changing those ingredients— they will caramelize, grow more concentrated, take on a hint of bitterness.

Do consider other factors to determine what bread will best serve your sandwich. Is the filling lacking crunch or does it need a bit more texture? OK, perhaps toasting the bread will be work.

Need even more texture? Choose a crustier bread. Conversely, do you want a smoothness that you bite with your tongue, as happens with a peanut butter and jelly sandwich? Then opt for a soft sliced white bread. Do the filling ingredients require a stronger bread with greater structure? For example, a meatball sandwich can't possibly be made on that soft sliced white—it would soak through, making the bread unappetizingly soggy. And the heavy meatballs would rip up the bread, leaving a mess where the meal should be.

But just as supporting actors merit Oscars in their own right, so, too, does bread. It is *really* important to use good bread. We're not suggesting that some common breads do not have their place; they may be perfect for barbecue or for a grilled cheese sandwich. But in general, when you're making the sandwiches in this book, use good bread. In our recipes, we list the type of bread to use for each sandwich. But if you have trouble finding some of these breads, substitute one that you will enjoy and that's similar in style. A good multipurpose, neutral French country loaf will pretty much get the job done.

We strongly recommend, therefore, that you buy your bread at a bakery. It need not be an artisanal bakery, and it really need not be fancy bread to be fresh and good. But even the most modest bakeries tend to have great fresh bread. If stopping at a bakery is not feasible, you can do what many hotels and restaurants do: order parbaked frozen breads online. These breads have been slightly underbaked and flash-frozen; you simply bake them for about 15 minutes and they taste and feel almost as good as home-baked. And speaking of home-baked, bread machines make home baking a relatively quick, easy, and viable option.

Remember, any bread that goes stale quickly is going to be good because it is not loaded with preservatives. But do not fear that this means you'll be throwing away unused bread. As we mention in our section on buying (see page 62), bread freezes very well. Keep out what you'll use, freeze the rest, and then toast it as you go. With a baguette, slightly moisten the crust, wrap the bread in foil, heat it in the oven, and it will emerge fresh again.

Too much bread in a sandwich is as problematic as too flavorful or too textured a bread. It can dwarf the other flavors and make the sandwich too filling. The simple solution is to scoop out some of the innards of the bread.

And then there's the toasting to consider. Toasting changes two things besides the temperature: the texture and the flavor. You can decide when you want to add a bit of charring, or—if you're making something rustic and really flavorful—when the sandwich might benefit from being put directly on a burner over a low flame and burnt a bit around the edges.

This reminds us of an important distinction: Some recipes call for *toasted* bread while others call for *grilled,* with different end results. Toasting can be done not only in a toaster but also in a toaster oven or a conventional oven. Toasting adds texture by relatively slowly and uniformly browning the bread. In a few recipes we instruct that the bread be toasted on one side only and that side placed inward, leaving the untoasted, softer side on the outside of the sandwich. Grilling, on the other hand, is done in direct contact with higher heat, on a grill, in a grill pan, or in a cast-iron skillet. While the texture changes, it does so a lot less than when bread is toasted, as the bread does not have a chance to get crisp. Grilling exposes the bread to high heat for a short time. This leaves its internal texture mostly unchanged while altering the taste, adding harmonizing bass notes and smokiness. We say that grilling the bread "charcoalizes" it—it may not be a standard term, but we think it best describes what happens.

And here's a final point, about knives: buy the cheapest good bread knife you can find, because they are impossible to sharpen. As soon as the knife grows dull, just buy a new one.

stewed apricots and fennel with ricotta, pistachios, and black pepper

A cheese-and-fruit Danish, the Austro-Hungarian apricot dumpling called *Marillenknödel,* a Turkish dessert of poached dried apricots with sweet-tangy cream and pistachios . . . some flavor combinations just work well, across cultures and continents. This especially pretty open-faced sandwich is great for breakfast, brunch, a light lunch, an afternoon snack, even a dessert; it's sweet but not too sweet. The colors, tastes, and textures of puffy white ricotta, velvety golden apricots, silky syrupy ribbons of fennel, crunchy toasted green pistachios, and a grinding or two of black pepper on top create a surprise for the palate and a feast for the eye. We both love putting a big platter of these sandwiches in the middle of the table and watching them disappear.

Use slightly underripe apricots; you can stew them longer than riper fruit and so they will absorb more of the flavors of the spices. Other stone fruits such as plums work well, too. The stewed fruit can be prepared in advance and kept refrigerated in its own syrup for several days. **MAKES 4 OPEN-FACED SANDWICHES**

1 cup water

1 cup sugar

2 cinnamon sticks

4 star anise

¼ teaspoon black peppercorns, roughly crushed

6 fresh apricots, pitted and quartered

½ bulb fennel, sliced crosswise into ⅛-inch strips

4 slices country bread

½ pound ricotta cheese

2 tablespoons chopped toasted pistachios

Sea salt and freshly ground black pepper

In a saucepan, combine the water, sugar, cinnamon, star anise, and crushed peppercorns and bring to a boil. Reduce the heat and simmer for 2 minutes. Add the apricots and fennel, and stir. Bring the mixture back to a simmer and cook for about 10 minutes, until the apricots are soft and the fennel has just a slight crunch.

Grill the bread on both sides. Spread the ricotta on each slice of bread and top with the apricots and the fennel. Finish with the pistachios and season with salt and pepper. Cut into halves, and serve.

coolsandwiches

goat cheese with avocado, celery, walnut pesto, and watercress

8 tablespoons fresh goat cheese (chèvre)

8 slices hearty multigrain bread

1 cup sliced celery (about ¼ inch thick)

4 tablespoons Lemon Vinaigrette (page 180)

2 cups watercress, largest stems removed

1 ripe avocado, halved, pitted, peeled, and sliced

Kosher salt and freshly ground black pepper

2 tablespoons Walnut Pesto (page 197)

This sandwich was inspired by a salad of avocado and celery that Sisha grew up eating in his native Chile. Popular in Chile, where avocados are plentiful (they're sold by the bagful at stoplights for a song), the salad is dressed with lemon juice and olive oil; folks often add walnuts as well. And so we've adapted these elements to a sandwich that balances the creaminess of the avocado with the crunch of the celery, the "high notes" of the lemon with the "bass note" of a walnut pesto. We tossed in some watercress as well, to add some pepperiness. A great summer-time sandwich, it's easy to eat, both in the sense that it's not at all messy and in the sense that while substantial, the sandwich is also light. **MAKES 4 OPEN-FACED SANDWICHES**

Spread the goat cheese evenly over 4 of the slices of bread. In a bowl, toss the celery in the vinaigrette, and place on top of the goat cheese. Add the watercress to the bowl used to dress the celery and toss with the remaining vinaigrette. Top the celery with the avocado, season with salt and pepper, and follow with the dressed watercress. Spread the pesto evenly over the 4 remaining bread slices. Close the sandwiches, cut into halves, and serve.

boucheron with grapefruit and crispy olives

We came up with this as a canapé for a party and had a hit on our hands; it's utterly simple and elegant. Boucheron combines the tartness, chalkiness, creaminess, and pungency that are the hallmarks of different goat cheeses for a beautiful balance of flavor and texture. Served open-faced on delicate bread as a finger sandwich or a canapé, this is dainty and easy to eat, but it can also be grilled as a sandwich if you want something hot and just a little bit oozy. **MAKES 8 BRUSCHETTE (2 PER PERSON)**

Preheat the oven to 350°F.

Heat the oil in a heavy skillet over medium-high heat. Add the olives and toss. Transfer the skillet to the oven and roast the olives for about 25 minutes, until very crisp. Meanwhile, bring the cheese to room temperature (if refrigerated) and cut the grapefruit into supremes (see Note). Lightly toast the bread slices. Gently crush the olives with the side of a knife. Slice and evenly spread the softened cheese on each slice of bread. Top with the grapefruit and olives and garnish with a few thyme leaves. Serve two bruschette per person.

1 teaspoon extra-virgin olive oil

⅓ cup pitted Niçoise olives

¼ pound Boucheron cheese

1 large grapefruit

8 slices baguette, cut on the bias

1 sprig fresh thyme, leaves picked

NOTE To cut a grapefruit into supremes, cut off the top and bottom of the fruit. With the grapefruit sitting on one of the cut sides, remove the peel and pith with a sharp knife, one section at a time. Insert the knife between the membrane and the fruit segment on both sides, at a 45-degree angle. Gently scoop out the segment and remove any seeds. Repeat for each fruit segment.

egg salad with caviar

4 extra-large eggs, preferably
pasture-raised

2 tablespoons finely chopped
celery

1 tablespoon finely chopped
red onion

2 tablespoons extra-virgin
olive oil

2 teaspoons chopped chives,
plus additional for garnish

½ teaspoon kosher salt

Freshly ground white pepper

¼ teaspoon white wine vinegar

1 teaspoon finely chopped
chervil, plus additional
for garnish

1 teaspoon finely chopped dill,
plus additional for garnish

4 slices brioche, ¼ inch thick,
3 inches square

2 teaspoons crème fraîche

4 teaspoons caviar or
salmon roe

Caviar is often garnished with hard-boiled eggs, so why not the reverse? To enhance the taste of the eggs, cook them until the yolks are still a bit soft so they can serve as the basis for the sauce. (This obviates the need for mayo, which would mask the eggs' flavor.) As this dish is all about the egg, use fresh farm eggs if possible. And if you wish to keep the price down, inexpensive salmon roe will substitute well for the caviar—and it looks beautiful, too. **MAKES 4 OPEN-FACED SANDWICHES**

Carefully lower the eggs into a saucepan of boiling water. Reduce the heat to an even boil and cook for 8 minutes. Remove from the heat and transfer the eggs to an ice-water bath. When the eggs have cooled completely, peel, add to a medium bowl, and roughly chop with a fork. Add the celery, onion, oil, chives, salt, pepper, vinegar, chervil, and dill and mix well.

Evenly distribute the egg salad on the slices of brioche. For neat and clean edges, cut off the crusts and cut each slice in half, straight across. Top each slice with the crème fraîche and the caviar. Garnish with the reserved chives, chervil, and dill, and serve.

chopped chickpeas with roasted peppers, black olives, lemon confit, and parsley

Our regulars love this bright and flavorful vegan sandwich, especially in summer. It's light yet absolutely satisfying. We like to cook our own chickpeas, but you can use canned—the chickpeas are a great vehicle for all of the vibrant flavors of the marinade. The red peppers provide a sweet counterpoint to the chickpeas; if you have the time, forgo the ones in the jar and roast your own (page 184). Then we add a low note (the Niçoise olives), and a high one (the confit), and finally the parsley (using whole leaves, not just a sprinkle). A final hint: toast the bread (just on the insides of the sandwich) for the perfect texture inside and out. **MAKES 4 SANDWICHES**

2 cups Marinated Chickpeas (page 196)

8 slices country bread

½ cup Roasted Peppers (page 184)

4 tablespoons pitted and chopped Niçoise olives

12 slices Lemon Confit (page 200)

1 cup flat-leaf parsley leaves

Freshly ground black pepper

In a food processor, coarsely chop the chickpeas, until they're spreadable but still chunky. Evenly spread the chickpeas over 4 of the bread slices. Top with the roasted peppers, olives, confit, and parsley, in that order, and season with pepper. Top with the remaining 4 slices of bread, cut into halves, and serve.

pan-fried eggplant with buffalo mozzarella, white anchovies, and raisin-pinenut relish

1 large eggplant, cut into 12 rounds

Kosher salt

1 cup extra-virgin olive oil

8 slices country bread

1 garlic clove, peeled

½ pound buffalo or regular mozzarella, cut into 12 slices

4 ounces (16 small fillets) white anchovies, marinated in vinegar and olive oil (not salt-cured), such as boquerones or alici

Raisin-Pinenut Relish (page 194)

Eggplant is like a sponge, soaking up whatever moisture it encounters. This, at least in part, is why it is typically breaded when fried—the bread crumbs serve as a shield to limit how much oil is absorbed. In this recipe, however, we salt the eggplant for about an hour to remove excess moisture and then fry it without a coating so it absorbs some oil. Decadent? Absolutely; the eggplant becomes luxuriously creamy and custardy. As buffalo mozzarella is a bit milder and softer than regular mozzarella, it is a perfect complement to the eggplant, but you can use whichever mozzarella you prefer. Interestingly, both the eggplant and the cheese are really the supporting cast in this sandwich; it is the relish that's the star. The secret ingredient? Anchovies. If you need a purely vegetarian sandwich, leave them out, but they lend a subtle kick, and with the sweetness of the raisins and texture of the pinenuts, you have a picante and assertive relish. **MAKES 4 SANDWICHES**

Distribute the eggplant on a sheet pan in one layer and generously salt on both sides. Lay another sheet pan on top of the eggplant and place a heavy object on top to add pressure. Set aside for 1 hour. Remove the weight and transfer the eggplant to paper towels and pat dry.

Add the oil to a large hot skillet, making sure to cover the entire bottom of the pan with about ⅛ inch of oil. Add the eggplant just before the oil starts to smoke—it should sizzle as the eggplant is dropped in and the eggplant should brown pretty quickly. Once the eggplant is golden on both sides, about 3 to 5 minutes, remove from the oil and transfer to paper towels. Allow the eggplant to come to room temperature or to cool completely.

Grill the bread slices on one side only. Rub the grilled side of 4 of the slices with the garlic. Top with the eggplant, followed by the mozzarella, the anchovies, and the relish. Top with the remaining 4 slices, cut into halves, and serve.

on buying: adventures in the food aisle . . . and beyond

Great food is prepared with great ingredients. It's an ethic we live by at 'wichcraft, and we're lucky to have farmers and suppliers who truck their food to us daily. Here in New York City, the greenmarkets offer city dwellers the same high-quality produce, fish, and meat that was once available only to people who lived close to farms and farmstands.

City people, who generally have small kitchens and limited storage space, are used to picking up only what they will need for a day's meal at a time. Often they shop as Europeans do: to a bakery for fresh bread, a butcher for meat, a greengrocer for produce. But what about those of you who don't have access to a farmstand or greenmarket? Or unlimited time? High-end supermarkets like Whole Foods offer products that are worth the trip and the higher prices. Many major supermarkets like Wegman's now offer quality "shops" with finer products, too. There are in-store butchers and fishmongers who are knowledgeable and happy to special-order items, usually at no additional cost. But whatever your supermarket, get to know the people behind the meat and fish counters and tell them exactly what you're looking for—they will procure other cuts of meat or types of fish if you ask, and they will steer you to the freshest food. Also, with a bit of planning, you can purchase high-quality ingredients online if you don't mind paying for shipping (see Resources). And if you can carve out a little time for one trip beyond the supermarket, find a decent bakery.

Great ingredients don't come cheap. If budget is a consideration, buy the best you can afford, in smaller quantities. This is where the humble sandwich is your friend; 3 ounces of roasted pasture-raised chicken layered with mozzarella and pesto on great bread will taste a lot better than 8 ounces of bargain chicken breast or processed deli meat at roughly the same cost—or at least not for appreciably more money. And, frankly, we as a society are in the habit of overstuffing our sandwiches, so you're not sacrificing anything by buying a bit less; if anything, you are safeguarding your health as well as conserving your money.

If you're pressed for time you have options. Most supermarkets offer an extensive selection of condiments, like chutneys and mustards. If you don't have time for the full recipe, cut corners here so that you can still roast the vegetables or braise the meat that is the foundation of the sandwich. See "Pantry Provisions," page 188, for items to keep stocked in your kitchen.

Eating well doesn't just involve a commitment to buying food differently than you may have in the past. It also means thinking about food seasonally, much the way good restaurants do. You'll never see a B.L.T. on the menu at 'wichcraft in the winter months. Sure, there may be perfect-looking red tomatoes trucked up from Mexico, but most likely they've been picked unripe to withstand travel and don't taste like much. We'd rather leave the sandwich off the menu altogether in the winter months than sacrifice the flavor. We urge you to do the same. Go to the store and see what is fresh and flavorful and *then* plan your menu.

Of course, there are a few exceptions to this rule. Peas are a spring vegetable, but fresh peas can be hard to find and, frankly, frozen peas taste great and can be used throughout the year. Ditto for canned tomatoes, which are terrific for condiments and sauces regardless of the season. In these cases, try to buy organic, as the food tends to be prepared in smaller quantities and with greater attention to flavor.

We are proud of the relationships we've forged with our purveyors and of our ability to work with fresh, seasonal products grown locally or procured ethically and with care. No matter what your locale or your means, you can adopt good shopping habits that result in your putting fresher, healthier, and tastier food on your table, without having to sell the farm to do so.

raw yellow beets with avocado, grapefruit, and radish sprouts

2 medium yellow beets, peeled and julienned

1 tablespoon plus a drizzle of extra-virgin olive oil

Juice from ½ lemon

1 teaspoon kosher salt, plus extra for seasoning

Freshly ground black pepper

1 large grapefruit

1 ripe avocado, halved, pitted, peeled, and thinly sliced

8 slices Pullman bread, crusts removed

1 cup loosely packed radish sprouts

Left uncooked, beets are not only crunchy and refreshing but also surprisingly substantial, making a satisfying base for this sandwich. Radish sprouts add a bit of heat as a counterpoint. And the avocado adds the needed element of richness. **MAKES 4 SANDWICHES**

In a bowl, toss the beets in 1 tablespoon of the oil, the lemon juice, 1 teaspoon of the salt, and pepper to taste and set aside until ready to use. Cut the grapefruit into supremes (see Note, page 55).

Evenly layer the avocado slices on 4 of the slices of bread. Drizzle some oil on the avocado and season with salt and pepper. Top with the grapefruit, yellow beets, and radish sprouts. Place the remaining 4 slices on top, cut into halves, and serve.

smoked salmon with avocado, green mango, and basil

We use unripe mango here as one would a vegetable. Be sure that the mango is still hard to the touch (you should not be able to put a dimple in it) so you can then julienne it. Adding a bit of lime enhances the mango's freshness. **MAKES 4 SANDWICHES**

In a bowl, toss the mango in the lime juice and season with salt. Lightly toast the bread.

Place the avocado on 4 slices of the bread and gently mash and spread with a fork. Drizzle the avocado with the oil and season with pepper. Top with the mango, smoked salmon, and basil. Add the top slices, cut the sandwiches into halves or quarters, and serve.

1 small unripe mango, peeled and julienned

Juice from ½ lime

Kosher salt

8 thin slices Pullman white bread

1 ripe avocado, halved, pitted, peeled, and sliced

Drizzle of extra-virgin olive oil

Freshly ground black pepper

8 ounces smoked salmon, thinly sliced

12 to 16 basil leaves

marinated white anchovies with soft-cooked egg, roasted onions, salsa verde, and frisée

8 ounces (32 small fillets)
white anchovies, marinated
in vinegar and olive oil (not
salt-cured), such as
boquerones or alici

4 large eggs, preferably
pasture-raised

2 cups frisée lettuce

2 teaspoons extra-virgin
olive oil

1 teaspoon red wine vinegar

Kosher salt

8 slices country bread

Freshly ground black pepper

½ cup Roasted Onions
(page 182)

4 tablespoons Salsa Verde
(page 199)

Anchovies usually play a supporting role in a dish, typecast as the salty accent. But we just love them, so we challenged ourselves to craft a sandwich that actually features them. We knew that if we succeeded, we'd have a sandwich that could have a small but faithful following. And so it came to pass. We adapted an interesting Scandinavian preparation that paired anchovies with eggs—the richness of the eggs balances the tartness of the fish. We liked it. And, as it turns out, so does that small (but ever-growing) band of devotees we'd envisioned. **MAKES 4 SANDWICHES**

Place the anchovies on paper towels to drain excess oil. Carefully lower the eggs into a saucepan of boiling water. After 7 minutes, remove the eggs and place in an ice-water bath. Once cool, carefully peel. (The whites should be cooked through and the yolks should be soft, almost runny.)

In a bowl, toss the lettuce in the oil and vinegar and add salt to taste. Lightly toast the bread on one side only.

Place one egg on the toasted side of 4 slices of bread and gently mash and spread out with a fork. Season the eggs with salt and pepper. Top the eggs with the onions, followed by the anchovies and the frisée. Spread an even coat of salsa verde on the toasted side of the 4 top slices of bread. Close the sandwiches, cut into halves, and serve.

sicilian tuna with fennel, black olives, and lemon

What self-respecting sandwich shop doesn't carry a tuna sandwich? We admit that we almost didn't. But when a magazine wanted to do an impromptu photo shoot before we opened, we had to improvise with ingredients already on hand at Craftbar. We seized a can of Sicilian tuna and added a few other items—and when we tasted the sandwich after the shoot, we realized we had a winner.

Let go of the traditional tuna with lots of mayo—the mayonnaise masks the taste, a pity when using good tuna. Instead, use just a bit of lemon-flavored mayo on the bread, and season the tuna with lighter ingredients, such as the fronds of the fennel, similar in texture to dill but lending a fresher flavor to the fish. **MAKES 3 TO 4 SANDWICHES**

TO MAKE THE TUNA SALAD, combine all the ingredients in a bowl, and mix well. Adjust the seasoning as necessary and refrigerate until ready to use.

TO MAKE THE MARINATED FENNEL, remove the stalks from the fennel and reserve the fronds. Using a mandoline slicer or sharp knife, thinly slice the fennel crosswise starting from the top. In a bowl, toss the fennel slices in the oil, lemon juice, and reserved fennel fronds, and season with salt and pepper. Set aside at room temperature to marinate for 10 minutes.

Split the baguette lengthwise. Spread the mayonnaise evenly across the bottom slice and layer with the tuna salad, fennel, olives, confit, and fennel fronds. Drizzle some of the oil from the confit on the inside of the top slice of the baguette. Close the sandwiches, cut into three or four equal pieces, and serve.

FOR THE TUNA SALAD

2 (6-ounce) cans yellowfin or albacore tuna, drained

2 tablespoons extra-virgin olive oil

2 teaspoons red wine vinegar

2 tablespoons finely diced red onion

1 tablespoon capers, drained

2 teaspoons chopped fresh oregano, or 1 teaspoon dried Sicilian oregano

Kosher salt and freshly ground black pepper

FOR THE MARINATED FENNEL

1 medium bulb (about ½ pound) fennel

2 tablespoons extra-virgin olive oil

1 tablespoon lemon juice

Kosher salt and freshly ground black pepper

1 baguette

3 tablespoons Lemon Mayonnaise (page 178) (optional)

4 tablespoons pitted and chopped Niçoise olives

12 slices Lemon Confit (page 200)

lobster with sweet potato–fennel slaw and tarragon vinaigrette

2 (1½-pound) lobsters, tails and claws only

8 tablespoons extra-virgin olive oil

2 cups peeled and julienned sweet potato

2 teaspoons kosher salt, plus extra for seasoning

2 tablespoons chopped fresh tarragon

4 tablespoons chopped green onions (white part only)

4 teaspoons white wine vinegar

Freshly ground black pepper

2 cups very thinly sliced fennel

8 slices country bread

Lobster and sweet potato: a seemingly odd couple, we know, but they have in common great textures, beautiful color, and a certain sweetness. Knowing that tarragon and lobster is a classic combination, we dress the sweet potato with a tarragon vinaigrette; the fennel adds a complementary fresh taste. **MAKES 4 SANDWICHES**

In a large pot, bring a generous amount of water to a boil. Cook the lobster tails for 7 minutes and the claws for 9 minutes. Immediately submerge the lobster in ice water. When cooled, crack the shells and remove the meat. Cut the meat into small chunks and set aside.

Add 3 tablespoons of the oil to a large skillet over high heat. Add the sweet potato, season with 2 teaspoons of the salt, and sauté for 2 to 3 minutes, until golden. In a large bowl, combine the tarragon, green onions, remaining 5 tablespoons oil, and the vinegar and mix well. Season with salt and pepper. Toss the lobster in the vinaigrette. Add the fennel and the sweet potato, and season with salt and pepper as necessary.

Grill the bread on both sides. Top 4 slices of bread with the lobster salad, add the top slices, and close the sandwiches. Cut into halves and serve.

roasted shrimp salad with tomatoes and olives

With no boiled shrimp and no mayo, this shrimp salad is immediately set apart from its traditional counterpart. It's actually closer to a scampi sandwich. Eschewing the mayo keeps the contents light and the flavor assertive. Throwing a party? As the shrimp are particularly beautiful, this recipe could also be used to make canapés. **MAKES 4 OPEN-FACED SANDWICHES**

Add 2 tablespoons of the oil and the sliced garlic to a large skillet placed over medium-high heat. Once the garlic is fragrant, add the shrimp and season with salt and pepper. Add the red pepper flakes and sauté for about 5 minutes, until the shrimp are cooked through. Pour the white wine into the skillet and stir to dissolve bits stuck to pan. Remove the pan from the heat. Transfer the shrimp to a bowl and set aside to cool.

Combine the shrimp with the tomatoes, olives, parsley, dill, green onions, lemon zest and juice, the remaining ½ cup oil, and the oregano. Season with salt and pepper, if necessary.

Grill the bread on both sides and lightly rub with the garlic clove. Place the shrimp salad on top and serve open-faced.

2 tablespoons plus ½ cup extra-virgin olive oil

1 tablespoon thinly sliced garlic plus 1 (peeled) clove

1 pound peeled and deveined shrimp

Kosher salt and freshly ground black pepper

½ teaspoon red pepper flakes

¼ cup white wine

1 cup cherry or grape tomatoes, quartered

¼ cup pitted Niçoise olives, roughly chopped

¼ cup chopped flat-leaf parsley

¼ cup chopped fresh dill

¼ cup chopped green onions (white parts only)

Zest and juice from 1 lemon

1 tablespoon chopped fresh oregano, or ½ tablespoon dried Sicilian oregano

4 slices multigrain bread

marinated fresh tuna with green beans, pickled peppers, garlic, and mayonnaise

1 pound yellowfin tuna steak, about 1 inch thick

Kosher salt and freshly ground black pepper

1 tablespoon vegetable oil

6 peppadew or hot Italian pickled peppers, finely chopped

1 small shallot, thinly sliced

½ cup extra-virgin olive oil

¼ cup thinly sliced basil leaves

2 teaspoons sherry vinegar

1 tablespoon finely chopped black olives

2 cups green beans, trimmed

8 slices country bread

1 garlic clove, peeled

4 tablespoons Mayonnaise (page 176)

Let it not be said that we didn't warn you: this is a five-napkin sandwich, tasty and light but also juicy and messy, making it great outdoor summer fare. When buying the ingredients, remember that fresh tuna should be deep red, so if it's turning brown or gray don't buy it. Playfully sweet and hot, peppadew peppers are perfect for the marinade; if you can't find them, substitute pickled cherry peppers so that you retain sweetness in addition to bite. Placing it on the cutting board with the raw side up and cutting from the top down keeps the tuna from falling apart when you cut it . . . no promises from us that it will be as considerate when you bite into it a few minutes later! **MAKES 4 SANDWICHES**

Season the tuna generously with salt and pepper. Add the vegetable oil to a large cast-iron skillet placed over high heat. Add the tuna and sear on one side only until the steak is cooked halfway through (cook it less if you prefer your tuna rare or more if you prefer it well done). Remove from the heat and set aside, seared side down.

In a small bowl, combine the peppers, shallot, olive oil, basil, vinegar, olives, ½ teaspoon of salt, and pepper to taste and mix well.

With the seared side down, cut the tuna into ¼-inch slices. Transfer the tuna to a rimmed plate and cover with the marinade. Refrigerate for 30 minutes, basting the fish every few minutes with any marinade that gathers on the bottom of the plate.

Submerge the beans in a pot of boiling water and cook for 5 minutes. Remove from the heat and drain. Using your hands, split the beans in half lengthwise and set aside.

Grill the bread on one side only. Lightly rub the garlic on the grilled side of 4 slices and top with the marinated tuna, followed by the beans. Spread the toasted side of the top halves with the mayonnaise. Close the sandwiches, cut into halves, and serve.

salads: for those of you who just don't "do" bread

Odds are, if you're reading a sandwich cookbook you're not averse to cooking with carbs. But if you are, or if you wish to prepare food for a low-carb-loving loved one, the answers you seek may still lie in sandwich recipes. This is because nearly any sandwich recipe can be adapted to yield a satisfying salad.

And so, at 'wichcraft we offer patrons the option of ordering any of our sandwiches as a salad instead. We replace the bread with salad greens (and occasionally make a few other modifications, as we explain here). If chosen correctly, the lettuce can supply the texture and crunch that bread would have provided. We shun mesclun and microgreens in favor of baby lettuces, which are tender and delicate but still have good texture. While customers opt for salad versions of many of our sandwiches, we are amazed at others they ask us to adapt, such as grilled cheese! The thought of melting cheese over greens instead of bread doesn't move us, but it does show that, just as they say there's someone out there for everyone, pretty much every sandwich can be enjoyed in salad form by someone.

Salads are similar to sandwiches in that they provide a meal with consistent taste throughout. In both, the textures and flavors must be balanced, which may require adapting a recipe beyond simple replacement of bread with greens, but it is generally quite easy to make the transition. Here are a few considerations to keep in mind when adapting a sandwich to be eaten as a salad:

- If the sandwich recipe has mayonnaise or mustard, or another condiment incompatible with salad eating, you need to find elements for the dressing or an ingredient that will accomplish the same goals (e.g., adding sweetness, acidity, or richness). For example, when we adapt our turkey sandwich to a salad, we do not use the aïoli; instead we use Lemon Vinaigrette (page 180).

- The bread may have served as a mellowing agent. Without it, you may find that the sandwich flavors are out of balance, with too much lemon confit or too overpowering a presence of olives, or it may now be too salty or acidic. You need to adjust the amount of ingredients accordingly. No matter what dressing you choose, consider lightly dressing all of the ingredients as well, so that everything is uniformly and properly seasoned.

- While you can pre-assemble many (though by no means all) sandwiches, you cannot do the same with salads. You can put together many of the components in advance, but they cannot be dressed too early without wilting. Similarly, you must be wary of certain ingredients that wilt the lettuces—ingredients with oil, for example. Further, certain ingredients will self-destruct too far in advance for other reasons. For example, one of our recipes involves candied walnuts, but if you add them too soon and refrigerate the salad, the walnuts will lose their crunch and be soggy and unappealing. So such ingredients should be set aside to be added at the last moment.

- Temperature also wilts greens. Meats that are warm in our sandwiches are served cold in our salads. Another option is to select a green that can withstand some wilting, such as frisée or spinach. For example, our Fried Eggs with Bacon, Gorgonzola, and Frisée (page 30) also makes a terrific—and popular—salad.

- Like Emily Post, we advocate bite-size greens that do not require a knife to be eaten, but we do so

for reasons epicurean rather than of etiquette. Sure, those large leaves of romaine can look quite dramatic fanned out on the plate, but you can't possibly get an even coat of dressing on them; instead, the dressing pools in the creases. Conversely, we do not recommend going to the opposite extreme with the chopped salad. While some are quite good, choose to make one carefully. Chopping lettuce that aggressively bruises it, causing it to "bleed," which has a most unappetizing effect. Good greens are generally somewhat delicate and you don't want to chop them to bits for the same reason you don't put an onion in a food processor: you wind up with a soupy mess. The argument in favor of a chopped salad is that it mixes the flavors, but you can achieve that by having all the ingredients cut to the right size and mixing them well.

One last note: People tend to be judicious when composing a standard meal or its portable version, a sandwich, selecting components that balance one another. Yet they tend to throw all thought to the wind when making a salad, tossing in eleven or twelve ingredients so as to feel they've eaten a hearty meal. Not only is there no need to do so, but we ask you to resist the urge. Fewer ingredients on the salad plate, each chosen for its interplay with the others, provide balance and contrast—you can actually taste what you've selected. So approach salads as you approach sandwiches—as meals worth composing with thought, creativity, and pleasure.

chicken salad with walnuts, roasted tomatoes, pickled red onions, and frisée

Do you know anyone who does *not* make chicken salad with leftover chicken? We don't. And folks tend to want mayonnaise, some fruity sweetness and/or nuts, crunch, and texture. We're happy to oblige.

We start with our homemade Mayonnaise (page 176). And if you have not yet tried the Pickled Mustard Seeds (page 187), this chicken salad gives you the perfect excuse. We're not sure "pickled" is the perfect term for them—they're flavored with sugar, vinegar, and water and puff up, caviar-like. This gives the chicken salad little bubbles that pop as you eat it, as caviar does, releasing a lightly mustardy flavor. The Pickled Red Onions (page 190) lend sweet, sour, and oniony flavors, as well as texture and crunch. Frisée adds texture as well. And using Roasted Tomatoes (page 195)—a staple in our own home kitchens—makes this sandwich a year-round choice. **MAKES 4 SANDWICHES**

Kosher salt

2 sprigs fresh thyme

2 sprigs fresh rosemary

2 bay leaves

Freshly ground black pepper

1 pound boneless chicken breast

½ cup diced celery

¼ cup chopped walnuts

¼ cup Pickled Mustard Seeds (page 187), strained

½ cup Mayonnaise (page 176)

1 tablespoon lemon juice

2 cups frisée lettuce

½ tablespoon extra-virgin olive oil

½ teaspoon red wine vinegar

½ cup Roasted Tomatoes (page 195), chopped

8 slices multigrain bread

¼ cup Pickled Red Onions (see page 190)

In a pot, bring about 2 quarts of water to a gentle simmer and salt heavily so it tastes like seawater. Add the thyme, rosemary, bay leaves, and 1 teaspoon pepper. Add the chicken to the poaching liquid and simmer gently until it reaches an internal temperature of 160°F. Allow the chicken to cool in the liquid and remove when ready to use.

Dice the chicken. In a bowl, combine with the celery, walnuts, mustard seeds, mayonnaise, and lemon juice and season with salt and pepper.

In a bowl, toss the frisée in the oil and vinegar, and season with salt and pepper. Distribute the tomatoes on 4 slices of bread. Top with the chicken salad, followed by the onions and the frisée. Top with remaining bread slices, cut into halves, and serve.

chicken liver pâté with fried onions and radish salad

FOR THE PÂTÉ

8 ounces chicken livers

2 tablespoons unsalted butter

2 small shallots, finely chopped

Kosher salt and freshly ground black pepper

1 tablespoon Cognac

2 tablespoons heavy cream

FOR THE FRIED ONIONS

1 cup thinly sliced yellow onion

2 tablespoons white wine vinegar

4 cups vegetable oil

2 cups all-purpose flour

Kosher salt

FOR THE RADISH SALAD

6 medium radishes

2 tablespoons prepared or freshly grated horseradish

2 teaspoons extra-virgin olive oil

1 teaspoon white wine vinegar

3 teaspoons Dijon mustard

1 teaspoon chopped parsley

Kosher salt and freshly ground black pepper

8 slices challah or Pullman white bread

2 teaspoons Dijon mustard

The fried onions in this recipe are sliced very thin and coated with flour to make them crisp. We wanted them to be a bit tart, but the more customary buttermilk just didn't take the onions where we wanted them to go. So we first soak the onions in vinegar, then flour and fry them; this way they have the acidity we were after. (Think salt-and-vinegar potato chips.) The radish salad adds some heat to the equation, balancing the ensemble. **MAKES 4 SANDWICHES**

TO MAKE THE PÂTÉ, with a paring knife, remove any fat, veins, and membranes from the livers. Rinse the livers under cold water until the water runs clear, and place on paper towels. In a large heavy-bottomed skillet over medium heat, add the butter and shallots, and sauté until golden. Season the livers with salt and pepper and add to the skillet. Sauté on both sides for about 5 minutes. Add the Cognac, stir, and cook for another minute or so until the alcohol has evaporated. Remove from the heat and set aside to cool.

Add the livers, including the pan juices, to a food processor and pulse until blended. Add the cream and blend until smooth. Season with salt and pepper. To make a very fine pâté, press the mixture through a sieve; for coarser pâté, use as is. Transfer the pâté to a container. (Any leftovers will keep in the refrigerator for 1 week.)

TO MAKE THE FRIED ONIONS, in a bowl, combine the onion and vinegar, and set aside for 10 minutes. Fill a large heavy-bottomed pot with the vegetable oil. Heat the oil to a temperature of 350–360°F. The oil is ready when you can see it moving around in the pot; test with a small piece of onion, making sure that the oil sizzles when the onion is added. Drain the onion and dip into the flour, shaking off any excess. Working in batches, fry the onion in the oil until golden and crisp, about 1 minute. Using a slotted spoon, transfer the onion to paper towels and season with salt.

TO MAKE THE RADISH SALAD, julienne or roughly grate the radishes and place in a medium bowl. Add the horseradish, oil, vinegar, mustard, and parsley and mix well. Season with salt and pepper.

Toast the bread slices on both sides. Evenly spread the pâté on 4 slices, and spread mustard on the other 4 slices. Top the pâté with the radish salad, followed by the fried onions. Top with the mustard-coated slices, cut the sandwiches into halves, and serve.

salami with marinated cauliflower and bitter greens

While this sandwich is not one of our top sellers, it has its fervent followers, like those of the anchovy sandwich (see page 68). Taking our inspiration from the traditional New Orleans muffaletta—the sandwich of salty meats and tangy olive salad on a thick round roll—we often pair a fresh smoked salami similar to a sopressata with a drier saucisson sec. But you can customize your sandwich for your palate with your own favorites: prosciutto, mortadella, pancetta—any salami will stand up nicely to the myriad flavors that burst from the marinated cauliflower salad. Don't let the name *cauliflower* dissuade you—this is not the boiled bane of your childhood. Rather, it's a textured mix of tastes in a bold marinade, with raisins and caraway seeds. **MAKES 4 SANDWICHES**

Remove any green leaves from the cauliflower while keeping the stem. Quarter, and using a sharp knife or the slicing attachment on a food processor, slice the cauliflower as thin as possible. (Don't worry if some of the cauliflower crumbles into small pieces.) In a bowl, combine the cauliflower with all the marinade ingredients and mix well. Set aside to marinate for 6 hours or more. Make sure to stir the mixture from the bottom before using.

Slice the ciabatta rolls in half, with a thicker bottom half (see Note). Place the marinated cauliflower on the bottom slices and top with the salami and the bitter greens. Spread the mustard evenly on the top slices and close the sandwiches. Cut into halves and serve.

MARINATED CAULIFLOWER

1 medium head cauliflower

¼ red onion, finely chopped

1 teaspoon finely chopped garlic

½ cup small golden raisins

3 tablespoons capers, drained

Pinch of red pepper flakes

2 teaspoons caraway seeds, toasted

½ cup flat-leaf parsley, finely chopped

4 teaspoons chopped fresh oregano, or 2 teaspoons dried Sicilian oregano

1 cup extra-virgin olive oil

⅓ cup white wine vinegar

2 teaspoons kosher salt

Freshly ground black pepper

4 soft ciabatta rolls

½ pound salami or saucisson sec, thinly sliced

2 cups loosely packed bitter greens, such as dandelions, beet greens, or mustard greens

4 teaspoons Dijon mustard

NOTE Cut the bottom of the bread a bit thicker than usual, and then make the salad your bottom layer, so that the marinade soaks into the bread.

flatiron steak with cucumber and ginger salad and black chile mayonnaise

1 pound flatiron or sirloin steak

Kosher salt and freshly ground black pepper

1 teaspoon vegetable oil

4 ciabatta rolls

4 tablespoons Black Chile Mayonnaise (page 177)

2 cups peeled, cored, and julienned English cucumber

2 tablespoons peeled and julienned fresh ginger

1 cup cilantro leaves

Juice of 1 lime

In steak sandwiches, the meat is usually paired with onions, cheese, or similarly rich flavors. We wanted something lighter and brighter, something, say, that a person might opt for at lunchtime without needing to nap afterwards. And so we use fresh ginger (which we julienne like a vegetable rather than shred, mince, grate, or sprinkle as a spice) and cucumber, both very refreshing. While Black Chile Mayonnaise (page 177) does add a touch of richness, this is still a very light red meat sandwich. **MAKES 4 SANDWICHES**

Season the meat with salt and pepper. Heat the oil in a large cast-iron skillet over high heat. Add the steak and sear for about 5 minutes on each side. Remove from the heat and set aside to rest for 5 minutes. Thinly slice the meat against the grain.

Slice the ciabatta rolls in half and scoop out as much bread as possible. Spread the mayonnaise on the top halves of the rolls. Layer the sliced meat on the bottom halves and top with a generous amount of the cucumber, ginger, and cilantro. Drizzle the lime juice on top and season with salt. Close the sandwiches, cut into halves, and serve.

mortadella with grilled radicchio and pistachio vinaigrette

Please do not let the bad bologna sandwiches of your youth deter you from trying this sandwich. Good mortadella is silky, flavorful, and because it doesn't require aging, usually far more affordable than most artisanal sandwich meats. Here, we balance the smooth texture and rich taste of mortadella with the bitterness of grilled radicchio. The Pistachio Vinaigrette (page 181) is a nod to the classic use of pistachios embedded in the meat. **MAKES 4 SANDWICHES**

1 small head radicchio

1 tablespoon extra-virgin olive oil

Kosher salt and freshly ground black pepper

1 baguette

¾ pound mortadella, thinly sliced

Drizzle of Pistachio Vinaigrette (page 181)

Cut the radicchio in half and then each half into four pieces. In a bowl, coat the radicchio with the oil and season with salt and pepper. In a grill pan or a cast-iron skillet over high heat, grill the radicchio for about 5 minutes, until it's wilted and slightly charred.

Cut the baguette into 4 pieces and slice each of them in half. Place the mortadella on the bottom halves and top with the radicchio and the Pistachio Vinaigrette. Close the sandwiches and serve.

bacon, lettuce, and tomato with mayonnaise

This American classic is available at deli counters year-round, but at 'wichcraft, it's a seasonal sandwich served only when local tomatoes are at their peak. For us, this is a tomato sandwich, with crisp bacon (be sure it's good quality!) and Bibb lettuce serving almost as condiments. We use a thick slice of tomato, say ½ inch, well seasoned with sea salt, really good pepper, and even a little olive oil. This is one of the sandwiches for which architecture matters, so please pay attention to the assembly instructions. For a special kick, rub a peeled garlic clove over the bread before assembling. A mix of heirloom tomatoes is ideal, combining colors and tones, sweetness and acidity. Imagine a slice of red plum, a slice of green zebra, and a slice of German yellow: summer in a sandwich. **MAKES 4 SANDWICHES**

1 pound thick-cut bacon

8 slices country bread

4 tablespoons Mayonnaise (page 176)

1 pound ripe heirloom or beefsteak tomatoes, sliced into ½-inch rounds (see Note)

Sea salt and freshly ground black pepper

4 large leaves of Bibb lettuce

NOTE Sit the tomato stem side down on the counter and using a very sharp knife, slice it horizontally to prevent the juices from running out.

In a heavy skillet, over medium-high heat, cook the bacon until golden brown and crisp on both sides. Transfer to paper towels to drain. Toast the bread on one side only. Evenly spread the mayonnaise on the toasted side of 4 slices of bread. Place the tomatoes on top of the mayo, making sure that the slices don't overlap and the surface of the bread is covered. Season the tomatoes with salt and pepper. Place the bacon over the tomatoes, followed by the lettuce. Close the sandwiches with the remaining 4 bread slices, toasted side down. Carefully cut into halves and serve.

roast beef with grilled red onions, radish slaw, and black pepper mayonnaise

FOR THE ROAST BEEF

1 pound boneless beef, eye round

½ tablespoon kosher salt

1 tablespoon coarsely ground black pepper

FOR THE RADISH SLAW

½ pound daikon radish, peeled and julienned or shredded

1½ tablespoons white wine vinegar

1 teaspoon kosher salt

1 teaspoon sugar

1 tablespoon extra-virgin olive oil

1 tablespoon prepared horseradish

½ tablespoon chopped flat-leaf parsley

Freshly ground black pepper

4 ciabatta rolls

4 tablespoons Mayonnaise (page 176), made with beef drippings instead of water

½ cup Grilled Red Onions (page 190)

4 small radishes, thinly sliced

Here's one for a party: Roast a large piece of beef and feed a big crowd. If your gathering is in the backyard, toss the onions in the marinade and grill them until they're a little bit charred. But if you are cooking the onions indoors, roast them in a cast-iron skillet until they start to caramelize. The radish slaw—a mix of daikon and red radishes with a little bit of horseradish (a traditional condiment for roast beef)—contributes crunchy, spicy coolness.

The mayo, though, is the genius of the sandwich. When you order a roast beef sandwich at a restaurant, you always hope it will come *au jus*—everyone loves to dip into those delicious flavors. Well, as 'wichcraft sandwiches are often eaten on the go, we let the beef rest after we roast it and then use the drippings in the mayo. You get the flavor of the dip without the drip (although, admittedly, this is still a three- or four-napkin sandwich). **MAKES 4 SANDWICHES**

Preheat the oven to 325°F.

TO MAKE THE ROAST BEEF, pat the meat dry and rub with the salt and pepper. In a hot ovenproof skillet, sear the meat until browned all over. Transfer to the oven and roast for about 30 minutes, until it reaches an internal temperature of 120°F. Remove the meat from the oven and transfer to a plate. Set aside to rest and cool completely, ideally overnight. Collect any juices from the skillet, and reserve 1 to 2 tablespoons for the mayonnaise. If needed, add some water to the skillet, stir, and reserve additional juices.

TO MAKE THE RADISH SLAW, in a medium bowl, toss the daikon radish in the vinegar, salt, and sugar and marinate at room temperature for 1 hour. Place the daikon in a strainer and drain for

30 minutes. Transfer to a bowl and toss in the oil, horseradish, parsley, and pepper.

Cut the ciabatta rolls in half and thinly slice the roast beef. Spread the mayonnaise on the bottom halves and top with the roast beef, onions, radish slaw, and sliced radishes. Close the sandwiches, cut into halves, and serve.

warmsandwiches

,,,

fontina with black trumpet mushrooms and truffle fondue

2 ounces dried black trumpet
mushrooms

1 teaspoon extra-virgin
olive oil

Kosher salt and freshly ground
black pepper

1 teaspoon chopped garlic

1 teaspoon chopped fresh
rosemary

1 tablespoon unsalted butter

16 slices fontina cheese

8 slices Pullman white bread

4 teaspoons white truffle
fondue, or a light drizzle of
truffle oil

NOTE If you don't have a
sandwich press, you can grill
the sandwiches in a hot
skillet. Brush the outside of
the sandwich with a little olive
oil and place in the hot pan
over medium-high heat. Press
the sandwich by placing
another heavy pan on top and
reduce the heat to medium-
low. When the bottom of the
sandwich is golden and crusty,
and the cheese has started to
melt, flip the sandwich and
grill on the other side.

This delicate little indulgence makes a marvelous treat; cut up into little squares, it's perfect party fare. We were already considering creating a grilled cheese sandwich with fontina when one of our purveyors came to us with the white truffle fondue. Unlike many truffle oil products, this fondue is made with real truffles. We tried it . . . and loved it. It is the ideal complement to the mellow flavor of fontina and the fresh Pullman bread. We wanted to add some sautéed mushrooms, and chose the black trumpets for their low moisture content and springy texture. If you find them fresh—which can be difficult, even in season—rinse them well to get rid of all the grit. **MAKES 4 SANDWICHES**

Soak the dried mushrooms in lukewarm water for about 30 minutes, until fully reconstituted. Drain and with your hands, squeeze to remove as much water as possible. Transfer to a large plate or sur-face to air-dry. Heat the oil in a medium skillet until hot, add the mushrooms, and season with salt and pepper. Sauté for about 2 min-utes, then add the garlic and rosemary, and sauté for another min-ute. Add the butter and stir until fully incorporated, making sure not to brown the butter too much. Remove from the heat and set aside.

Preheat a sandwich press according to the manufacturer's specifi-cations (see Note).

Place 2 slices of fontina on each of 4 slices of bread and spread the truffle fondue evenly on top of the cheese (or drizzle lightly with truf-fle oil). Top with the mushrooms and the other 2 slices of fontina. Close the sandwiches and place in the sandwich press (no need to butter the press or the bread). Close the lid and apply slight pres-sure. Cook without disturbing for 5 to 8 minutes. Open the press and check for color and temperature: the cheese should be melted and the bread golden. If the bread is sticking to the press, allow it to cook for a bit longer and it will unstick itself. If the press seems to generate more heat on the bottom, flip the sandwich halfway through to ensure even cooking (making sure the ridges in the bread line up). Once cooked, remove, cut into halves, and serve.

gruyère with caramelized onions

16 slices Gruyère cheese

8 slices rye bread

1 cup Roasted Onions (page 182)

This is one of Tom's favorites, one that showcases how a sandwich can be adapted from a meal. The meal here is French onion soup. Whereas in the soup the onion is the star, with the crouton and cheese to support it, in the sandwich we flip that: the onions serve as the relish. We roast the onions very slowly, caramelizing them, until dark golden brown to balance the assertive and pungent Gruyère. With the rye bread to hint at the Alsatian origin of the soup, we end with something rustic and homey, and yet something that, unlike soup, can be enjoyed while walking down the street. **MAKES 4 SANDWICHES**

Preheat a sandwich press according to the manufacturer's specifications (see Note, page 96). Place 2 slices of cheese on each of 4 slices of bread. Follow with a generous amount of onions and the other 2 slices of cheese. Close the sandwiches and place in the sandwich press (no need to butter the press or the bread). Close the lid and apply slight pressure. Cook without disturbing for 5 to 8 minutes. Open the press and check for color and temperature: the cheese should be melted and the bread golden. If the bread is sticking to the press, allow it to cook for a bit longer and it will unstick itself. If the press seems to generate more heat on the bottom, flip the sandwich halfway through to ensure even cooking (making sure the ridges in the bread line up). Once cooked, remove, cut into halves, and serve.

roasted asparagus with red onions, basil, and vacherin

This sandwich came about in our favorite way: by visiting the greenmarket, picking up the cheese, and then meandering through the farmers' stands to see what fresh offerings might be paired with it. It was June; we came away with beautiful asparagus, red onions, basil, and a rustic bread—all the fixins for an open-faced sandwich on the grill. (If you don't have an outdoor grill, you can use a grill pan.) Thinking back to the days when cooks in diners put hubcaps atop burgers as they cooked, to steam them a bit, we recommend either closing the grill or inverting a metal bowl over the sandwich to keep the heat in and help melt the cheese.

By the way, if you can't find or do not care for Vacherin, substitute any good melting cheese. **MAKES 4 OPEN-FACED SANDWICHES**

1 small bunch pencil asparagus, bottoms trimmed

1 small red onion, sliced into ¼-inch rings

2 tablespoons extra-virgin olive oil

Kosher salt and freshly ground black pepper

2 tablespoons sherry vinegar

4 basil leaves, roughly chopped

4 slices rustic country bread

1 garlic clove, peeled

½ pound Vacherin cheese, sliced

1 sprig fresh thyme, leaves picked

In a bowl, combine the asparagus and onion, and toss in the oil. Season with salt and pepper. Place the asparagus and onion on a grill or in a hot grill pan and cook until slightly charred, 5 to 10 minutes. Return the asparagus and onion to a mixing bowl, toss in the vinegar and basil, and set aside.

Grill the bread until golden brown on one side only. Remove and lightly rub the toasted side with the garlic. Top the garlic toast with the asparagus and onion, and follow with the cheese. Place the open-faced sandwiches on the grill, cover, and remove when the cheese is just starting to melt. Garnish with the thyme. Cut each sandwich in half and serve.

cheddar with smoked ham, poached pear, and mustard

While we use a delicious aged Cheddar, this sandwich will be a success with other cheeses, too, as long as they have a big presence, such as a sharp Gouda (no subtle fontinas or mozzarellas); because the cheese is the star of the sandwich, it needs to stand up to the other flavors. Use just enough smoked ham to balance the cheese and poached pear. Use a very thin layer of mustard on the bread, right next to the cheese. The bread in this instance should be something nutty and fruity. The tartness of the dried cranberries in our bread is a great addition to the sandwich, so if you don't have them in your bread, you could add them to the poaching liquid when you prepare the pears. **MAKES 4 SANDWICHES**

⅔ cup sugar

⅔ cup cider vinegar

1 piece star anise

1 teaspoon black peppercorns

2 whole cloves

Pinch of ground peperoncino or red pepper flakes

½ cinnamon stick

2 Bartlett pears, peeled, cored, and cut into ⅛-inch slices

8 slices sharp Vermont Cheddar cheese

8 slices cranberry-pecan bread

8 slices smoked ham

¼ cup Spiced Walnuts (page 199) if cranberry-pecan bread isn't available (optional)

Freshly ground black pepper

2 teaspoons Dijon mustard

In a saucepan, combine the sugar, vinegar, ⅔ cup water, star anise, peppercorns, cloves, peperoncino, and cinnamon stick, and bring to a boil. Reduce the heat and simmer for 15 minutes. Add the pears, bring back to a simmer, and cook for 2 to 3 minutes, until tender. Remove from the heat and cool in the liquid. Unless used right away, transfer the pears and juices to a container. (Keeps in the refrigerator for 1 to 2 weeks.)

Preheat a sandwich press according to the manufacturer's specifications (see Note, page 96). Place 1 slice of cheese on each of 4 slices of bread. Top with the ham, followed by 4 to 6 slices of pear and the walnuts, if using. Season with pepper and top with the remaining cheese. Spread the mustard on the remaining slices of bread, close the sandwiches, and place in the sandwich press (no need to butter the press or the bread). Close the lid and apply slight pressure. Cook without disturbing for 5 to 8 minutes. Open the press and check for color and temperature: the cheese should be melted and the bread golden. If the bread is sticking to the press, allow it to cook for a bit longer and it will unstick itself. If the press seems to generate more heat on the bottom, flip the sandwich halfway through to ensure even cooking (making sure the ridges in the bread line up). Once cooked, remove, cut into halves, and serve.

mozzarella and provolone with roasted tomatoes and black olives

8 ounces fresh mozzarella, thinly sliced

8 slices country bread

4 tablespoons Roasted Tomatoes (page 195), chopped

4 tablespoons pitted and chopped Niçoise olives

½ teaspoon dried Sicilian oregano

4 slices aged provolone

This sandwich was a real crowd-pleaser when it was on the 'wichcraft menu, popular with adults and kids alike. Why? Probably because it tastes like pizza! We prepare it as a pressed sandwich, but it also works beautifully grilled in a pan with a little olive oil, or if you don't want to add any fat, heat it open-faced in the oven until the cheeses melt. The mozzarella is milky and gooey, with a great mouth feel, and the provolone adds personality. Roasting tomatoes concentrates their flavor and caramelizes their sugars; it's a great way of getting the best of a tomato when it's not at the height of the season.

When herbs are a primary ingredient, only fresh will do. But when they are used as a seasoning, as in this sandwich, dried work very well. One way to ensure you have high-quality dried herbs is to dry them yourself. Take a bunch of fresh oregano, tie it up at the stem end, and hang it upside down to dry, outside if possible, but wherever there is plenty of air circulation. When the herbs are thoroughly dry and the leaves fall off the stems at the touch, crumble the leaves, store them in a jar, and use them as long as the flavor remains strong and pleasing, about 2 months.

MAKES 4 SANDWICHES

Preheat a sandwich press according to the manufacturer's specifications (see Note, page 96). Divide the mozzarella among 4 bread slices. Spread the tomatoes and the olives evenly over the mozzarella. Sprinkle with the oregano and top with the provolone. Close the sandwiches with the remaining bread slices and place in the sandwich press (no need to butter the press or the bread). Close the lid and apply slight pressure. Cook without disturbing for 5 to

8 minutes. Open the press and check for color and temperature: the cheese should be melted and the bread golden. If the bread is sticking to the press, allow it to cook for a bit longer and it will unstick itself. If the press seems to generate more heat on the bottom, flip the sandwich halfway through to ensure even cooking (making sure the ridges in the bread line up). Once cooked, remove, cut into halves, and serve.

the fresh air fund internship program

As the parents among you can attest, it's hard to get your kids to eat their vegetables and downright impossible to get your teens to do anything you want them to. Now imagine getting three headstrong adolescents not only to forgo their fries in favor of frisée, but to be excited enough about it to try to inspire others to do the same.

That's exactly what we did last summer. It was the second season of 'wichcraft's internship program in partnership with the Fresh Air Fund (FAF). Founded in 1877, FAF is a not-for-profit agency that provides free summer vacations and summer camp in rural areas to children from New York City's more disadvantaged areas. But it does more than that.

FAF also has a Career Awareness Program for adolescents. One aspect of this program is job shadowing, in which the participants spend a day or more at a business, experiencing its operations firsthand. What began as the desire of 'wichcraft managing partner Jeffrey Zurofsky to participate has developed into an intensive eight-week summer internship, the likes of which are unprecedented at FAF.

In the spring, we hold three or four open-call job shadowings. At each, roughly fifteen to twenty young people attend, learn about 'wichcraft's mission and business practices, and are invited to make two sandwiches from an array of ingredients: the first is a sandwich they love; the second is a sandwich composed of ingredients they have never before tried. We then press the sandwiches for them and they sit together, eat them, and share their thoughts about what they came up with. At the day's end, the participants are told about the summer internship program and are invited to apply. Those who submit cover letters and résumés undergo a rigorous interview process; three are hired for the eight-week, full-time, paid internship.

A week's orientation to the company is followed by two weeks in the kitchen learning all aspects of our process there. Another two weeks are spent in the store, learning the ins and outs of customer service, and behind the scenes with our operations and marketing folks. In the final three weeks, the interns have the opportunity to integrate their experiences via their final project: to create a sandwich that will go on the menu for a full year (something that we can be proud to offer our patrons). Last summer's challenge was to create a vegetarian sandwich. But not just any vegetarian sandwich—it had to appeal to meat eaters, to be a sandwich for the guy who wants the meatloaf.

These were not kids who knew a whole lot about vegetables. We took them to the greenmarket, to the vegetable markets, to a vegetarian restaurant, and after briefly considering the artichoke (too expensive, too seasonal, too difficult to prep), they landed on eggplant as the main element of their sandwich. That was a great idea, as eggplant is easy to obtain, economical, easy to work with, and substantial and meaty. The kids had to do extensive research on how eggplant is cooked in various cultures—Italy, the Middle East, parts of Asia. They were sent to the curry places on Lexington Avenue, to Little Italy, and to

Chinatown; and they returned, foods in hand, for tastings to establish how different flavors interact with eggplant. With our guidance, they began to develop their ingredients list, and it was off to the kitchen to start developing recipes.

As our interns worked, we oversaw the process, asking questions, offering suggestions, subtly influencing the direction the recipe took. We taught them to craft the sandwich as they'd compose an entrée, with the bread as just one of the ingredients. We asked them to think about flavors, about seasonality, about elements that work well together, about combinations people enjoy.

The teens had tremendous pride in what they created. They were also proud of the PowerPoint presentation they put together with our director of finance, which they presented to the board of directors of the Fresh Air Fund, along with a tasting. They learned that there is a lot behind the design of a sandwich; they also learned that there is a business side to what we do.

Whether they want to pursue a culinary career or not, these three fifteen-year-olds, who previously wouldn't touch a vegetable, expanded their aspirations along with their palates. Further, they have gained not only valuable knowledge and experience in the kitchen but also a broad skill set that is transferable to many other careers they may pursue. And our patrons gained—for a year, anyway—a sandwich of eggplant marinated in a tomato sauce with capers and fennel seeds, along with roasted peppers and a chickpea spread (see page 109).

marinated eggplant with chickpea puree, roasted peppers, and watercress

This sandwich was developed through our Fresh Air Fund Internship Program by three industrious and talented teens. See page 106 for the story behind the sandwich. **MAKES 4 SANDWICHES**

Distribute the eggplant on a sheet pan and salt generously on both sides. Lay another sheet pan on top of the eggplant and place a heavy object on top to add pressure. Set aside for 1 hour.

Heat 3 tablespoons of the oil in a heavy-bottomed skillet. Add the onion and cook for about 10 minutes over low heat without browning. Add the garlic, and once the garlic starts to brown, add the fennel seeds and capers, and cook until the capers start to open. In a blender, puree the tomatoes and their juice and add to the skillet. Season with pepper and simmer for about 20 minutes over medium heat.

Meanwhile, pat the eggplant dry and brush off any excess salt. Brush with a little olive oil and add to a large cast-iron skillet over medium-high heat. Cook the eggplant until tender but not soggy. Remove from the skillet and add to the tomato marinade while they are both hot. Add the herbs to the skillet, and season with pepper. Set aside and allow too cool.

Preheat the oven to 350°F.

In a blender or food processor, puree the marinated chickpeas until smooth. Slice the ciabatta rolls in half and distribute the marinated eggplant on each bottom half. Spread the chickpea puree on the top halves and top with the roasted peppers. Transfer to the oven and remove once the bread is toasted and the eggplant is warm. In a bowl, toss the watercress in 1 teaspoon olive oil and the vinegar, and season with salt and pepper. Place the watercress over the eggplant and close the sandwiches. Cut into halves and serve.

1 pound eggplant, cut into ¾-inch slices

Kosher salt

3 tablespoons plus 1 teaspoon extra-virgin olive oil, plus extra as needed

¼ cup thinly sliced yellow onion

1 garlic clove, thinly sliced

1 teaspoon fennel seeds

1 tablespoon capers, drained

1 (14-ounce) can Italian plum tomatoes

Freshly ground black pepper

6 basil leaves

¼ cup chopped flat-leaf parsley

½ cup Marinated Chickpeas (page 196)

4 ciabatta rolls

½ cup Roasted Peppers (page 184)

1 cup watercress

1 teaspoon balsamic vinegar

fried squid po-boy with avocado and black chile oil

1 pound small squid (bodies and tentacles), cleaned

3 lemons

Kosher salt

Vegetable oil for frying

All-purpose flour

1 ripe avocado, halved, pitted, peeled, and sliced

4 soft hero rolls, split

4 teaspoons Black Chile Oil (page 185)

What makes this sandwich particularly special is the chile oil, and for this we must give credit where it is due. Many years ago, Sisha worked with a talented chef named Neil Swidler. An Arizona native later working in New Orleans, Neil made this strikingly beautiful and fiery oil and shared the recipe with Sisha, who will be forever grateful. This sandwich, our homage to a New Orleans classic, is our way of saying thanks. The chiles, by the way, can be found in Whole Foods and specialty markets, as well as in Mexican bodegas everywhere. **MAKES 4 SANDWICHES**

Rinse the squid and cut the bodies into ¼-inch rounds. In a bowl, toss the squid in the juice from 1 lemon and season with salt. Fill an 8- to 10-inch skillet with enough vegetable oil to come about 2 inches up its side. Make sure the pot is deep enough to leave at least 4 inches above the oil. Heat the oil to 350–360°F. The oil is ready when you can see it moving around in the skillet; test with a small piece of squid, making sure that the oil sizzles when the squid is added. In a bowl, toss the squid in a generous amount of flour and shake off any excess. Working in batches, fry the squid until golden and crisp, about 2 to 3 minutes. Using a slotted spoon, transfer the squid to paper towels to drain. Sprinkle with salt.

Layer the avocado on the bottom half of each hero roll and coat the top halves with the chile oil. Stuff the rolls with the squid and squeeze a generous amount of juice from the remaining lemons on top. Close the sandwiches and serve.

tuna and roasted tomato melt

This is a straightforward version of the classic sandwich—with a few improvements. We opt for good-quality tuna, we use celery root instead of celery, and we roast the tomatoes to extract the most flavor. Since this is a warm sandwich, the roasted tomato actually holds up better than would its raw counterpart. We think you'll agree that the addition of the fresh oregano brings out the flavor of the cheese. **MAKES 8 OPEN-FACED SANDWICHES (2 PER PERSON)**

Preheat the oven to 350°F.

In a bowl, flake the tuna with a fork and combine with the celery root, onion, and 1 teaspoon oregano. Add the mayonnaise and lemon juice, and mix well.

Toast the English muffins and top each slice with the tomatoes, followed by the tuna salad and the cheese, and season with the oregano. Place the sandwiches in the oven and remove once the cheese is melted. Serve open-faced.

2 (6-ounce) cans tuna packed in olive oil, drained

¼ cup peeled and finely diced celery root

¼ cup finely diced red onion

1 teaspoon chopped fresh oregano, or ½ teaspoon dried Sicilian oregano, plus additional for seasoning

4 tablespoons Mayonnaise (page 176)

Juice from ½ lemon

4 English muffins

8 tablespoons chopped Roasted Tomatoes (page 195)

8 slices Gruyère cheese

roasted pumpkin with mozzarella and hazelnut brown butter

1 pound pumpkin or other winter squash, peeled, seeded, and cut into 4 pieces

2 tablespoons extra-virgin olive oil

Kosher salt and freshly ground black pepper

8 ounces fresh mozzarella, thinly sliced

8 slices Pullman white bread

4 teaspoons Hazelnut Brown Butter (page 181)

We developed this recipe for this cookbook and promptly vowed to place it on the menu in the coming fall. Loosely based on pumpkin ravioli, it is the sandwich equivalent of comfort food. **MAKES 4 SANDWICHES**

Preheat the oven to 350°F.

In a bowl, toss the pumpkin in 1 tablespoon of the oil and place on a sheet pan. Season the pumpkin with salt and pepper and place in the oven. Roast for about 30 minutes, until soft.

Preheat a sandwich press according to the manufacturer's specifications (see Note, page 96). Remove the pumpkin from the oven, add to a large bowl, and mash with a fork. Season with the remaining tablespoon of oil and salt and pepper to taste. Place a thin layer of mozzarella on 4 slices of bread. Top with an even spread of hazelnut butter, followed by a layer of pumpkin. Cover with the 4 remaining bread slices, and place in the sandwich press (no need to butter the press or the bread). Close the lid and apply slight pressure. Cook without disturbing for about 4 minutes. Open the press and check for color and temperature: the cheese should be melted and the bread golden. If the bread is sticking to the press, allow it to cook for a bit longer and it will unstick itself. If the press seems to generate more heat on the bottom, flip the sandwich halfway through to ensure even cooking (making sure the ridges in the bread line up). Once cooked, remove, cut into halves, and serve.

whipped salt cod with roasted peppers and parsley

The drying of meats and fish is the oldest method of preservation. Salt cod (cod that has been both salted and dried) has been around for 500 to 1,000 years, since European fishing fleets discovered the rich cod supplies of the north Atlantic. The result was widespread use of salted cod, as in *baccalà* (Italian), *bacalhau* (Portuguese), *klippfisk* (Scandinavian), *morue* (French), and *saltfiskur* (Icelandic).

Why go through the lengthy process of desalting a fish that you could buy fresh? Flavor, for starters; if cod were fresh ham, salt cod would be its prosciutto. And texture; salt cod is supple and chewier than fresh cod. A rare treat to eat, salt cod also happens to hold up well in a sandwich. We've opted for the traditional pairing of salt cod with roasted red peppers, whose sweetness is a natural fit with the cod. **MAKES 8 BRUSCHETTE (2 PER PERSON)**

Submerge the cod in cold water and refrigerate for a few hours. Change the water and continue soaking overnight.

Remove the soaked cod from the fridge and drain. In a medium pot, bring the milk, cod, and potatoes to a simmer and add the thyme and bay leaf. Cook until the potatoes are fork-tender. Remove from the heat, transfer the cod and potatoes to a food processor or mixing bowl, and discard the milk and herbs. Add the cream and blend or mash (with a fork) until smooth. Add 1 teaspoon oil and season with salt, if necessary. Set aside.

Preheat the oven to 350°F.

In a small bowl, combine the garlic, butter, a pinch of salt, and lemon juice. Using a spoon, mix the ingredients well until smooth.

Slice the baguette on the bias into 8 pieces. Spread the garlic butter on one side of each slice and toast on a rack in the oven. Remove and place the whipped salt cod on the buttered side of the bread, topped with the peppers and parsley. Drizzle with a little olive oil, season with pepper, and serve.

1 (8-ounce) piece salt cod

2 cups whole milk

½ pound Yukon Gold potatoes, peeled and cut into large dice

2 sprigs fresh thyme

1 bay leaf

5 tablespoons heavy cream

1 teaspoon extra-virgin olive oil, plus extra for drizzling

Kosher salt

2 teaspoons minced garlic

4 tablespoons (½ stick) unsalted butter, softened

¼ teaspoon lemon juice

1 baguette

8 tablespoons Roasted Peppers (page 184)

2 tablespoons flat-leaf parsley leaves

Freshly ground black pepper

fried cod with tomato salad and serrano mayonnaise

FOR THE TOMATO SALAD

2 large ripe tomatoes, cored

½ small yellow onion, julienned

2 tablespoons extra-virgin olive oil

2 teaspoons sherry vinegar

Kosher salt and freshly ground black pepper

¼ cup loosely packed flat-leaf parsley leaves

FOR THE FRIED COD

1 pound cod fillet, sliced on an angle into ½-inch cutlets

Kosher salt and freshly ground black pepper

1 cup all-purpose flour

1½ cups seltzer water

Vegetable oil for frying

4 soft kaiser rolls

4 tablespoons Mayonnaise (page 176)

4 teaspoons finely chopped serrano chile

This dish was inspired by one from Sisha's native Chile: a fried fish with a traditional tomato and onion salad. In Chile, the onion is not a condiment in the salad but, rather, an ingredient in its own right. So as not to be overpowered by so much raw onion, we "shock" the onion first; this blunts the thrust of the onion without sacrificing its texture. The sparkling water in the batter lends a tempura-like quality. And since the traditional Chilean green chile is unavailable here, we use serrano chiles—smaller and about five times hotter than jalapeños, but thin-walled and easy to use. **MAKES 4 SANDWICHES**

TO MAKE THE TOMATO SALAD, in a large pot, bring water to a boil and lower the whole tomatoes into the boiling water; leave for 5 seconds, then immediately transfer to an ice-water bath, chill completely, and drain. Peel off the skins. If the skins aren't coming off, place back in the boiling water for a couple of seconds more. Place the onion in the same boiling water and leave in for 15 to 30 seconds; drain and transfer to the ice-water bath. Allow the onion to sit in the bath for 15 minutes.

Cut the tomatoes in half crosswise, discard the juices and seeds, and chop into large chunks. Transfer to a bowl, add the onion, and mix well. Add the oil, vinegar, salt and pepper, and the parsley and toss.

TO MAKE THE FRIED COD, season the fish with salt and pepper. In a medium bowl, combine the flour and the seltzer, and whisk into a thin and smooth batter. Fill an 8- to 10-inch skillet with enough oil to measure about 2 inches up the side. Make sure the pot is deep enough to leave at least 4 inches above the oil. Heat the oil to 350–360°F. The oil is ready when you can see it moving around in the skillet; test the heat with a small piece of fish, making sure that the oil sizzles when the fish is added. Dip the fish into the batter and carefully place a couple of pieces of fish into the hot oil at a

time. (It's important not to crowd the pot.) Fry the fish until golden, about 8 minutes, and transfer to paper towels with a slotted spoon. Season with salt.

Slice and lightly toast the rolls. In a bowl, combine the mayonnaise and the chile, and spread evenly over the bottom slices of bread. Top the mayonnaise with the fried cod and place the tomato salad on the top slices of bread. Close the sandwiches, cut into halves, and serve.

chicken breast with roasted peppers, mozzarella, and spinach-basil pesto

We devised this sandwich partly to challenge ourselves. Usually prepared in advance of its use in a sandwich, chicken loses moisture by the time it arrives there. So we looked for a way to keep the chicken moist . . . and we found it. By slowly and gently poaching the chicken, and then storing it in the poaching liquid until it's used, we lock in the moisture. (Use this trick whenever you're preparing chicken for a picnic or for use in a salad—the chicken will be moist and delicious, and without oil, to boot. Further, you can use the poaching broth for soup simply by adding more water, some vegetables, and some of the chicken.) We serve this as a pressed sandwich, but it also works well served cold.
MAKES 4 SANDWICHES

¼ cup kosher salt

2 sprigs fresh thyme

2 sprigs fresh rosemary

2 bay leaves

1 teaspoon freshly ground black pepper

1 pound skinless and boneless chicken breast

8 slices sourdough bread

¼ cup Spinach-Basil Pesto (page 197)

½ cup Roasted Peppers (page 184), chopped

8 ounces fresh mozzarella or buffalo mozzarella, sliced

In a pot, bring 8 cups water to a gentle simmer and salt heavily (so it tastes like seawater). Add the thyme, rosemary, bay leaves, and pepper. Add the chicken to the poaching liquid and simmer until it reaches an internal temperature of 160°F. Allow the chicken to cool in the liquid and remove when ready to use.

Preheat a sandwich press according to the manufacturer's specifications (see Note, page 96). Thinly slice the chicken breasts and evenly distribute on each of 4 slices of bread. Spread the pesto on top of the chicken and top with the peppers and mozzarella. Top with the remaining 4 slices, and place in the sandwich press (no need to butter the press or the bread). Close the lid and apply slight pressure. Cook without disturbing for 5 to 8 minutes. Open the press and check for color and temperature: the cheese should be melted and the bread golden. If the bread is sticking to the press, allow it to cook for a bit longer and it will unstick itself. If the press seems to generate more heat on the bottom, flip the sandwich halfway through to ensure even cooking (making sure the ridges in the bread line up). Once cooked, remove, cut into halves, and serve.

roasted turkey with avocado, bacon, balsamic onion marmalade, and mayonnaise

6 fresh sage leaves

1 (3- to 4-pound) boneless turkey breast

2 tablespoons unsalted butter, softened

Kosher salt and freshly ground black pepper

12 slices bacon

4 ciabatta rolls

½ cup Balsamic Onion Marmalade (page 193)

1 ripe avocado, halved, pitted, peeled, and sliced

4 tablespoons Mayonnaise (page 176)

NOTE Don't cook the bacon over too high heat or the fat will burn. When you're done, save the fat you've rendered and store it in the freezer. The next time you're roasting some vegetables, toss some bacon fat in with them!

This recipe is one of our biggest sellers but, interestingly, each customer cites a different reason the sandwich is special. One says that she could eat the onion marmalade with a spoon for breakfast daily. Others can't say enough about the bacon. Tom applauds Sisha's decision to cut the turkey thicker, thus showcasing its moistness. This is an ensemble piece, with no clear headliner. While we use ciabatta, this sandwich would work as well on country bread, too. **MAKES 4 SANDWICHES**

Preheat the oven to 350°F.

Slide the sage leaves under the skin of the turkey breast and place the turkey on a sheet pan. Rub the skin with the butter and season generously with salt and pepper. Roast the turkey for 1 to 1½ hours, until it reaches an internal temperature of 165°F. Baste the meat with its juices throughout. (Keep in mind that the meat will continue to cook even after it's removed from the oven, so be careful not to cook it too long.) Allow the meat to rest before slicing, or cool completely.

In a heavy skillet over medium-high heat, cook the bacon until golden brown and crisp on both sides. Transfer to paper towels to drain.

Slice the ciabatta rolls in half. Place the turkey slices on the bottom halves and top with the marmalade. Place the bottom and top halves of the rolls in the 350°F oven and remove once the marmalade is heated through and the bread is toasted. Top the marmalade with the bacon, followed by the avocado. Evenly spread the mayonnaise on the top halves of the rolls. Close the sandwiches, cut into halves, and serve.

pork sausage with pickled grilled fennel, ricotta, and arugula

If you elect to make the sausage yourself, you need not have casings—simply make sausage patties instead. Conversely, if you're making a recipe that calls for patties and you're starting with sausages that are already in their casings, what's to stop you from simply ripping them open and removing the contents?

We think you'll be delighted with the results of grilling the fennel and then pickling it lightly. And while we generally encourage substituting ingredients to your own taste, consider sticking with the recommended arugula here. It adds just the right tenor of spice to this sandwich. **MAKES 4 SANDWICHES**

1 bulb fennel, halved and cut lengthwise into ¼-inch slices

5 teaspoons extra-virgin olive oil

Kosher salt and freshly ground black pepper

2 teaspoons white wine vinegar

1 pound bulk sweet Italian sausage (not in casing)

2 cups arugula

1 teaspoon balsamic vinegar

4 ciabatta rolls

8 ounces ricotta cheese

In a bowl, toss the fennel in 1 teaspoon of the oil and season with salt and pepper. Place the fennel on a grill or in a grill pan over high heat and cook until slightly charred, about 1 minute. Remove from the heat and transfer to a bowl. Add the white wine vinegar, toss, and set aside in room temperature to marinate for 1 hour or more.

Shape the sausage into four patties. Add 3 teaspoons of the oil to a large skillet over medium-high heat and cook for 5 minutes on each side. In a bowl, toss the arugula in the remaining 1 teaspoon oil and the balsamic vinegar, and season with salt and pepper.

Cut the ciabatta rolls in half. Place the fennel on the bottom halves, followed by the sausage patties. Top with the ricotta and arugula. Close the sandwiches and serve.

cured duck breast with caramelized apples and endive

½ magret duck breast

1½ teaspoons black peppercorns

1½ teaspoons coriander seeds

1½ teaspoons fennel seeds

1 small shallot, thinly sliced

1 large garlic clove, thinly sliced

2 tablespoons kosher salt

1 teaspoon plus 2 tablespoons sugar

1 teaspoon chopped fresh thyme

2 tablespoons unsalted butter

1 small apple, peeled, cored, quartered, and sliced

2 endive, leaves separated

8 slices dark multigrain bread

This sandwich was adapted directly from a meal Tom had developed years earlier for Gramercy Tavern. We cure the duck lightly, for about 24 hours, more for flavor than to remove moisture. Then it is cooked *verrrrrry* slowly, with the fat side down. It is particularly important in this recipe to use a heavy-bottomed pan so that the heat distributes evenly, and to cook the duck over a super-low heat in order to render the fat without overcooking the duck. Once it's cooked and you let it cool, you can slice it and use it in myriad ways—as an appetizer, in salad, on canapés. Note that because the duck's been cured, its flavor is now concentrated and a little goes a long way. We pair the duck with caramelized apples and endive, which provide sweetness, acidity, and just the right edge of bitterness. Felling extra-indulgent? Save the pan in which you cooked the duck and toast the bread in the fat! **MAKES 4 SANDWICHES**

If the duck breast has a lot of fat, cut it down to a ¼-inch-thick layer. Score the fat diagonally in both directions. In a dry and hot small skillet, toast 1 teaspoon of the peppercorns, 1 teaspoon of the coriander seeds, and 1 teaspoon of the fennel seeds for 2 to 3 minutes. Roughly crush the spices and add to a medium bowl. Add the shallot, garlic, salt, 1 teaspoon sugar, and thyme and mix well. Place half of the curing mixture on a sheet of plastic wrap. Top with the duck breast and spread the remaining curing mixture on top of the duck. Close tightly and wrap in another sheet of plastic. Place in the fridge to cure for 24 hours.

RECIPE CONTINUES

Remove the duck from the fridge and quickly rinse off the curing mixture under cold water. Pat dry. Roughly crush the remaining peppercorns and combine with the remaining coriander and fennel seeds. Rub the spices all over the duck breast (top and bottom), pressing the spices into the skin. Place the duck breast skin down in a large heavy-bottomed skillet over medium heat. Immediately reduce the heat to low. The duck should sizzle just slightly as the fat will start to render. Pay close attention and maintain that slight sizzle. If the skillet gets too hot or has certain hot spots, move it around or remove from the heat completely for a second or two and bring it back. Once the fat has rendered, about 20 minutes, flip the duck breast and sear for another 2 minutes or so on the other side, until medium cooked. Remove the duck from the skillet and set aside to rest. Discard any spice mixture left in the pan and reserve the pan.

In a medium heavy-bottomed skillet over medium-high heat, combine the remaining 2 tablespoons sugar and the butter and stir until caramelized. Add the apple and cook until soft and golden brown. Remove the apples from the skillet and set aside. Add the endive and cook until wilted and caramelized. If the pan seems dry, add some water to steam the endive. Remove from the heat and let cool.

Place the skillet used to sear the duck over medium-high heat. Add the bread and toast on one side only. Thinly slice the duck and place it on the toasted side of 4 slices of bread. Top with the apples and endive. Cover with the remaining 4 slices, toasted side down, and cut into halves before serving.

less really is more

For decades following its North American debut in the 1910s, the bagel was a standard 3 inches in diameter and approximately 140 calories. Today, that's a "mini-bagel," and standard bagels are typically 5 to 6 inches and a whopping 350 calories. Burgers have more than doubled in size as well. A single blueberry muffin can easily have more than 500 calories. The standard 10-inch dinner plate has been increased to 12 inches, and plates are heaped with food, both in homes and restaurants. For fun, check out the National Institutes of Health's "Portion Distortion" quizzes online, to see how our sense of portion proportion has shifted over the decades.

Of course, this applies to sandwiches as well.

With Dagwood Bumstead setting the standard back in the 1930s, Americans have become trained to equate quantity with value. We've grown accustomed to the overstuffed sandwich. Much of what we're perceiving as part of that value is simply filler: shredded lettuce and tasteless tomato in a sandwich, a heap of rice at a Chinese buffet, or a mound of French fries at a diner. All in all, it's simply more food than we should be eating.

A sandwich is a balanced and concentrated meal unto itself. Don't be fooled by the compact appearance of a sandwich. People always look at a properly proportioned sandwich and exclaim, "Oh, that's small!" But they're not thinking that after they've eaten it. Remember, we tend to eat a sandwich a lot faster than a plated meal. And eating fast doesn't give our stomach the time to let our brain know we've had enough. Were the same amount of food in an appropriate-sized sandwich to be served on a plate, there would be a lot of food there. Further, the meat in sand-wiches is often cured, which means it is very strong in flavor, and one should not be eating a half-pound of it at one sitting.

In keeping with this "less is more" strategy, add the mayo or cheese only if they serve a purpose and marry well with the other ingredients. Lest you think we're "anti-mayo," no, indeed. In fact, we offer a recipe for mayonnaise (see page 176), and you can rest assured we do so in the hopes that you'll make and use it. This reminds us: if you use store-bought mayonnaise in the recipes that call for mayo, you may need to adjust the recipe, as commercial mayonnaises tend to contain sugar, which can skew the overall flavor of the sandwich.

The question to ask yourself when considering mayonnaise, as with any ingredient, really, is this: if you took the bread away, would it still make sense to match these ingredients? If not (and unless the sandwich is a tuna melt—the exception that proves the rule), they shouldn't be in a sandwich. As with any other pantry item added to a sandwich to accent the more central ingredients and lend just that right amount of acid, sweetness, heat, or other dimension, mayo should make its way into a sandwich only if it has something—in its case, usually richness—to offer.

As we stress time and again throughout this book, conceptualize the meal, and you've conceptualized the sandwich. Just as a good meal is not about quantity, or about plating too many offerings at once, or about adding cheese, mayo, or such "fillers" as lettuce and tomato, we'd forgo all of these in a sandwich as well.

Sorry, Dagwood.

pastrami with sauerkraut, gruyère, and whole-grain mustard sauce

You'll recognize this sandwich as a Reuben—with a few adjustments. Chief among them: We believe that mustard is the perfect condiment to cut the salty, sweet richness of cured meats, so we've replaced the Reuben's more prosaic Russian dressing with an easy-to-make mustard sauce. Using really good pastrami sets the tone for the entire sandwich. While the meats you typically find in a supermarket are injected with water, an artisanal product is simply cured, then smoked with real wood chips, concentrating rather than diluting the flavors. And though the product is more expensive, you'll need far less of it. You can try this sandwich with corned beef, too, especially if you're in the mood for a milder and less smoky experience. **MAKES 4 SANDWICHES**

8 slices Gruyère cheese

8 slices rye bread

1 pound pastrami, sliced

4 tablespoons Whole-Grain Mustard Sauce (page 196)

1 cup sauerkraut, drained

Preheat a sandwich press to the manufacturer's specifications (see Note, page 96).

Place 1 slice of cheese on each of 4 slices of rye. Follow with the pastrami, mustard sauce, sauerkraut, and the other slices of cheese. Cover with the remaining bread slices and place in the sandwich press (no need to butter the press or the bread). Close the top lid and apply slight pressure. Cook without disturbing for 5 to 8 minutes. Open the press and check for color and temperature: the cheese should be melted and the bread golden. If the bread is sticking to the press, allow it to cook for a bit longer and it will unstick itself. If the press seems to generate more heat on the bottom, flip the sandwich halfway through to ensure even cooking (making sure the ridges in the bread line up). Once cooked, remove, cut into halves, and serve.

slow-roasted pork with red cabbage, jalapeños, and mustard

1 tablespoon caraway seeds

3 whole cloves

1 star anise

½ tablespoon black peppercorns

½ cup kosher salt

1 (1¼ to 1½ pounds) boneless pork shoulder

2 cups shredded or thinly sliced red cabbage

2 tablespoons extra-virgin olive oil

1 tablespoon red wine vinegar

4 ciabatta rolls

2 tablespoons Dijon mustard

1 large jalapeño pepper, thinly sliced

While there are twelve or thirteen sandwiches in this book that Tom calls "my absolute favorite," this one truly is Sisha's. We use the pork shoulder, a very flavorful cut that benefits from slow cooking—so slow, in fact, that we set the oven on the lowest setting and leave the pork cooking overnight, which breaks down the textures, develops the flavors, and renders a lot of the fat. For the amount of meat called for in this recipe, you can get the same great texture and flavor in about four hours.

This recipe has its origin in pork barbecue, which is often served with coleslaw. The cabbage in our sandwich—a nod to that side of slaw—is seasoned with olive oil and red wine vinegar. It is assertive and acidic, balancing the richness of the pork, while the jalapeños add a nice kick. Peppers vary in intensity—sometimes two slices are more than plenty while sometimes eight won't be enough—so be sure to taste-test yours before layering them on. **MAKES 4 SANDWICHES**

Preheat the oven to 250°F.

Combine the caraway, cloves, star anise, and peppercorns in a spice grinder and process until they have the coarseness of salt. Combine the spices with the salt.

Rub the pork vigorously with the spice mixture until completely covered. Any spice mixture that doesn't stick to the meat can be removed. Place the meat in a roasting pan, cover tightly, and cook in the oven for about 4 hours. The meat should be fork-tender and some of the fat should have rendered into the bottom of the pan. Transfer the meat to a plate and discard the fat from the pan.

Increase the oven heat to 350°F.

In a bowl, combine the cabbage, oil, and vinegar and season generously with salt and pepper. The cabbage should taste quite salty and tangy.

Slice the ciabatta rolls in half. Spread the mustard evenly across the bottom halves. Using a couple of forks, pull the roasted pork apart and distribute some on the bottom and top halves. Place the bread in the oven and remove when the bread is lightly toasted and the meat is heated through. Add the cabbage on the bottom halves and top with the jalapeño. Close the sandwiches, cut into halves, and serve.

roasted pork and coppa with pickled pepper relish and fontina

1 tablespoon caraway seeds

3 whole cloves

1 star anise

½ tablespoon black peppercorns

½ cup kosher salt

1 (1¼- to 1½-pound) boneless pork shoulder

8 slices fontina cheese

8 slices country bread

4 tablespoons Pickled Pepper Relish (page 187) or jarred Italian cherry peppers, drained

8 slices coppa or prosciutto

This recipe is based on a Cuban sandwich traditionally made with roast pork, ham, pickles, Swiss cheese, and mustard. We start with the same main ingredient—the pork. It can be a loin, a ham, even a shoulder, but it should be roasted so that it retains some texture. Then we ratchet things up. In place of the ham, we have coppa, which comes from the neck of the pig and is cured and dried like prosciutto. Standing in for the pickle, we have a pickled pepper relish. The sugar in the recipe cuts through the spiciness and acidity, rounding out the flavors in the relish. Instead of the Swiss cheese in a Cuban, we use fontina. We press the sandwich just as you would a Cuban, and presto! We have what we have nicknamed the Cubano-Italiano. **MAKES 4 SANDWICHES**

Preheat the oven to 250°F.

Combine the caraway, cloves, star anise, and peppercorns in a spice grinder and process until they have the coarseness of salt. Combine the spices with the salt.

Rub the pork vigorously with the spice mixture until it is completely covered. Any spice mixture that doesn't stick to the meat can be removed. Place the meat in a roasting pan, cover tightly, and cook in the oven for about 4 hours. The meat should be fork-tender and some of the fat should have rendered into the bottom of the pan. Once cooked, transfer the meat to a plate and discard the fat from the pan.

Preheat a sandwich press to the manufacturer's specifications (see Note, page 96). Pull some of the fork-tender meat apart into thin strips. Place 1 slice of fontina on 4 slices of bread. Top with the pork, relish, coppa, and the other slices of fontina. Cover with the remaining bread slices and place in the sandwich press (no need to butter the press or the bread). Close the lid and apply slight

pressure. Cook without disturbing for 5 to 8 minutes. Open the press and check for color and temperature: the cheese should be melted and the bread golden. If the bread is sticking to the press, allow it to cook for a bit longer and it will unstick itself. If the press seems to generate more heat on the bottom, flip the sandwich half-way through to ensure even cooking (making sure the ridges in the bread line up). Once cooked, remove, cut into halves, and serve.

meatloaf with cheddar, bacon, and tomato relish

½ medium yellow onion, diced

1 tablespoon extra-virgin olive oil

1 garlic clove, minced

2 pounds ground beef (85% lean)

2 large eggs, preferably pasture-raised

¾ cup fresh bread crumbs

1 tablespoon chopped fresh oregano, or ½ tablespoon dried Sicilian oregano

2 tablespoons Dijon mustard

2 teaspoons kosher salt

1 teaspoon freshly ground black pepper

2 tablespoons ketchup

12 slices bacon

4 ciabatta rolls

8 slices yellow Cheddar cheese

8 tablespoons Tomato Relish (see page 182)

While we provide a meatloaf recipe here, we know how particular people are about their meatloaf recipes, so feel free to use your own. You'll often want to make this sandwich with cold, leftover meatloaf, which is perfect because it's easier to slice. But how to heat it up without drying it out? This is where the liquid from the tomato relish comes in: put the meatloaf slices into the sauce and pop them into the microwave or oven. The meatloaf is gently heated, absorbing all the flavor and moisture of the sauce. Now just layer on some aged Cheddar, bacon, if you like, and the tomato relish, and you have a hearty sandwich—the ultimate comfort food. **MAKES 4 SANDWICHES**

Preheat the oven to 350°F.

In a skillet over medium heat, sauté the onion in the oil until golden. Add the garlic and sauté for 1 to 2 minutes (be careful not to burn the garlic). Remove from the heat and set aside to cool.

In a bowl, combine the beef, eggs, onion bread crumbs, oregano, mustard, salt, and pepper. Form a loaf (approximately 7 x 5 x 3 inches in size) and place it in a roasting pan. Cover the loaf evenly with the ketchup. Bake for about 1 hour, until it reaches an internal temperature of 145°F. Remove and allow to rest slightly, then cut into ½-inch slices.

In a heavy skillet over medium-high heat, cook the bacon until golden brown and crisp on both sides. Transfer to paper towels to drain.

Slice the ciabatta rolls in half. Top each bottom half with a slice of warm meatloaf and the cheese. Place the relish on the top halves and top with the bacon. Place all the roll pieces in the 350°F oven and remove once the cheese has melted and the relish is heated through. Close the sandwiches, cut into halves, and serve.

red wine–braised flank steak with roasted peppers, onions, and gruyère

3 tablespoons vegetable oil

1 pound flank steak

1 medium carrot, cut into large dice

½ white onion, cut into large dice

2 garlic cloves, quartered

2 to 3 cups red wine

2 large sprigs fresh thyme

2 teaspoons kosher salt

1 large red onion, sliced crosswise into ¾-inch wheels

8 tablespoons Roasted Peppers (page 184)

2 teaspoons extra-virgin olive oil

½ teaspoon sherry vinegar

4 ciabatta rolls

8 slices Gruyère cheese

This is a sandwich that was so good we had to take it off the menu! Conceptually similar to a cheese steak, it was offered as a pressed sandwich, and when too many people ordered it at once, we had a traffic jam on our premises. So while you can no longer find it at 'wichcraft, you can make it for yourself. Flank steak is wonderfully easy to work with because it's lean—there's no waste, and it has an excellent texture for braising.

There are many schools of thought about the right wine to cook with. Some advocate cooking with the best wine, or at least a wine that you would want to drink; others believe in using the cheapest wine available. We suggest going with the wine that you can afford to use for cooking or the one you have lying around. At home, whenever he has some leftover red wine at the end of a meal, if he doesn't drink it the next day, Sisha puts it in a container in the freezer. He keeps adding to that container, and when he needs wine for braising, there it is. The blend is never the same twice—and always good. **MAKES 4 SANDWICHES**

Preheat the oven to 350°F.

Choose a heavy-bottomed ovenproof skillet or Dutch oven that's large enough for the flank steak to lie flat but is as snug as possible. Add 2 tablespoons of the oil to the skillet over high heat. Once the oil starts to smoke, add the meat and cook for 5 to 7 minutes on each side, until deep brown in color. Remove the meat from the skillet and set the meat aside.

RECIPE CONTINUES

Add the carrot and onion to the skillet, followed by the garlic. Sauté the vegetables over medium-high heat until they start to brown but are still firm. Return the meat to the pan. Add the red wine—enough to come three-fourths of the way up the side of the meat. Add the thyme and 1 teaspoon of the salt, cover the skillet, and transfer to the oven. Braise the meat for about 2½ hours, until the meat can be pulled apart with a fork. Transfer the meat to a plate to rest and cool.

Reserve and strain the pan juices and pour into a saucepan. Over medium-low heat, reduce the juices until thickened (it should coat the back of a spoon). With two forks, separate the meat into chunky strings and roughly cut them crosswise into 2- to 3-inch pieces. Place the meat in the pot with the reduced juices and coat well.

Brush the red onion with the remaining 1 tablespoon vegetable oil. In a grill pan or cast-iron skillet over high heat, grill the red onion (without separating into individual rings) until charred on the outside and slightly cooked on the inside. Place in a bowl and separate into rings. Add the peppers, olive oil, sherry vinegar, and remaining 1 teaspoon salt and mix well.

Slice the ciabatta rolls in half. Place 1 slice of cheese on each bottom and top half. Arrange the meat on the bottom halves of the rolls and the onions and peppers on the top halves and place all the roll pieces in the 350°F oven. Remove once the cheese is melted. Close the sandwiches, cut into halves, and serve.

crisp pork belly with sweet and sour endive

The beauty of this recipe is its simplicity: pork and endive. The key is to not disturb the pork in the pan. Yes, it will stick. Let it; it'll unstick later and you'll have the satisfying crispness you were after. The endive, roasted first with smoked bacon, vinegar, and caraway seeds, serve almost as a condiment. **MAKES 4 SANDWICHES**

Preheat the oven to 350°F.

Season the meat with salt and pepper. Heat the oil in a large oven-proof skillet over medium heat. When the oil slides easily across the pan, add the meat, skin side down. Cook for about 15 minutes, until the skin is browned. Transfer the meat to a plate and pour off all but 2 tablespoons of the fat from the skillet.

Add the onion, carrots, celery, leek, and garlic to the skillet. Cook the vegetables, stirring occasionally, for about 20 minutes, until they are tender and beginning to brown. Return the meat to the skillet, skin side up, and add about 2 cups of chicken stock (it should surround the meat, not cover it). Bring the stock to a simmer, then transfer the skillet to the oven. Gently simmer the meat, uncovered, for 1 hour. Add the remaining cup of chicken stock and cook for another hour or so, until the pork is tender enough to cut with a fork. Remove the skillet from the oven and cool the meat in the braising liquid.

RECIPE CONTINUES

1½ pounds boneless pork belly, skin on

Kosher salt and freshly ground black pepper

1 tablespoon peanut oil

1 medium onion, coarsely chopped

2 carrots, coarsely chopped

2 celery stalks, coarsely chopped

1 leek (white part only), chopped

2 garlic cloves, peeled

About 3 cups chicken stock

¼ pound smoked bacon, cut into small dice

1 teaspoon caraway seeds

2 endive, leaves separated

2 teaspoons sugar

¼ cup balsamic vinegar

4 ciabatta rolls

4 teaspoons Dijon mustard

Increase the oven temperature to 400°F.

Remove the meat from the liquid and gently lift off and discard the skin. Use a small knife to separate any pieces of skin that don't come away from the fat easily. Remove a small piece (about 2 tablespoons) of the fat from the meat and render in another skillet over high heat. Cut the meat into ¼-inch slices and evenly distribute in the skillet with the rendered fat. Leave in the skillet until the bottom of the meat turns crisp. Transfer the skillet to the oven and cook for 10 minutes, then flip the pork and continue cooking for another 10 minutes, until crisp. Remove from the oven and transfer the meat to paper towels.

In another skillet over medium-high heat, add the bacon and render the fat. If not much fat is rendered, add some of the pork belly fat to the skillet. Add the caraway seeds and toss, then add the endive and sauté until browned and slightly wilted. Add the sugar to the bottom of the skillet. Once the sugar has dissolved and starts to caramelize, add the vinegar and season with pepper. Continue cooking until the vinegar is reduced and the endive are just slightly moist. Remove from the heat and set aside.

Slice the ciabatta rolls in half. Spread the mustard on the bottom halves. Top with slices of the pork belly, followed by the endive. Close the sandwiches and serve.

roasted pork loin with prunes, dandelion greens, and mustard

This is a great sandwich to make with leftovers (in this case, leftover pork loin). One of the key elements in this sandwich is the choice of greens. Dandelion greens are bitter, but balance the other flavors of prunes and mustard. If the greens are not to your liking, either try buying smaller-leafed dandelion greens (the larger the leaf, the more pronouncedly bitter) or substitute mustard greens or endive. **MAKES 4 SANDWICHES**

Preheat the oven to 375°F.

Season the pork loin with salt and pepper and cover evenly with the caraway seeds. In an ovenproof skillet over medium-high heat, add 2 teaspoons of the oil and brown the meat until golden brown on all sides. Transfer the meat to the oven and roast for 30 to 45 minutes, until it reaches an internal temperature of 145°F.

In a saucepan, bring 2 cups water to a boil. Add the prunes, and immediately remove the pan from the heat. Set aside for 15 minutes, then drain.

Remove the meat from the oven and transfer to a plate to rest. Discard the oil from the skillet and return the skillet to the stove. Over high heat, add the prunes, wine, and mustard. Reduce until the liquid becomes a sauce that coats the prunes; set aside. Add any juices that gathered from the resting meat to the prunes.

In another skillet over medium-high heat, add the remaining teaspoon of oil. Once the oil is hot, add the garlic and sauté until fragrant. Add the dandelion greens and season with salt and pepper. Once the greens are wilted, add the vinegar, toss, and remove from the heat.

Slice the pork as thin as possible and grill the bread on both sides. Top 4 of the slices of bread with the prunes and sliced pork and season with salt. Place the dandelion greens on top. Cover with remaining slices of bread, cut into halves, and serve.

1 pound boneless pork loin

Kosher salt and freshly ground black pepper

2 teaspoons caraway seeds

3 teaspoons extra-virgin olive oil

16 small pitted prunes

¼ cup white wine

2 teaspoons mustard

1 large garlic clove, thinly sliced

4 cups loosely packed dandelion greens (small leaves are less bitter), thick stems removed

1 teaspoon white wine vinegar

8 slices country bread

roasted leg of lamb with lemon confit, mustard greens, and black olive mayonnaise

14 slices Lemon Confit (page 200)

1 tablespoon chopped fresh oregano, or ½ tablespoon dried Sicilian oregano

2 teaspoons pitted and chopped black olives

1 to 1¼ pounds boned leg of lamb

Kosher salt and freshly ground black pepper

1 tablespoon extra-virgin olive oil

2 cups chopped and tightly packed red or green mustard greens (stalks removed)

4 ciabatta rolls

6 tablespoons Black Olive Mayonnaise (page 178)

Lamb is an underappreciated and underutilized meat. It's better for you than other red meats; it's generally raised under healthier, more humane, and more sustainable conditions; it's fragrant, lean, and tender; and it has that slightly funky quality that makes it interesting to work with. Here, we've rubbed it with chopped lemon confit and olives. While the recipe calls for oven-roasting, roasting it slowly on the grill would work beautifully, too. In keeping with the great tradition of day-after-holiday leftovers and sandwich making, we think Easter Monday is when you'll want to be eating this one. **MAKES 4 SANDWICHES**

Preheat the oven to 350°F.

Finely chop 6 slices of the confit and transfer to a bowl. Add the oregano and black olives, and mix well. Rub the lamb with the mixture and season with salt and pepper. Add the oil to a heavy-bottomed ovenproof skillet over medium-high heat. Add the seasoned meat, fatty side down, and reduce the heat to medium. Sear the meat until it has browned on the bottom. Scoop up any rub mixture that falls off the meat during cooking and place evenly back on top of the meat. Once the meat has the desired color, baste with the rendered fat and transfer to the oven, uncovered. Roast for about 35 minutes, until it has an internal temperature of 125°F. Remove and transfer the meat to a plate to rest for 10 to 15 minutes. Discard any excess oil from the skillet and set aside.

Place the skillet back on the stove over medium-high heat and add the mustard greens. Season with salt and pepper and stir for 1 to 2 minutes, until the greens start to wilt. Add the juices that have collected on the plate with the resting meat. Wilt the greens for another minute or so until they have absorbed the juices, and remove from the heat.

With a sharp knife, slice the meat as thin as possible. Slice the ciabatta rolls in half and evenly spread the mayonnaise on the bottom halves. Top the mayonnaise with the meat, followed by the remaining confit and the mustard greens. Drizzle any remaining juices from the meat on top of the greens. Close the sandwiches, cut into halves, and serve.

the evolution of the sandwich: from the fertile crescent to the ham'n'cheese croissant

Folks are quick to credit John Montagu, the Earl of Sandwich, with the invention of the portable food that has been given his name, but study reveals a far more ancient and loftier pedigree for this unpretentious meal. Historians agree that the first sandwich on record was crafted at a Passover Seder in the first century B.C.E., when the great sage Hillel the Elder placed charoset (a mixture of chopped apples, nuts, and wine) between two pieces of matzo (unleavened bread), creating what is known at today's Seder tables as a Hillel sandwich.

Fast-forward more than a thousand years. The next reference to this method of eating was in medieval times, when thick slices of stale bread were commonly used as trenchers on which food was eaten as we use dishes today. This was the forefather of the open-faced sandwich, but it was said that a man would have to be very hungry indeed to eat his own trencher, as it was stale, hard, and baked with unbolted flour (unlike the soft, delicious bread we layer with roast beef and enjoy *au jus* today). Instead, trenchers were often handed out as alms after a feast or tossed to a favorite dog. Luckily for its recipients, the trencher was leavened with yeast, so at least it absorbed the grease and sauces from the meal that had been layered atop it.

Throughout Europe and the Middle East, combinations of meat, cheese, fruits, and condiments tucked into breads or pastry were popular long before they had a name. In England in the sixteenth and seventeenth centuries, these handy meals were known simply as "bread and cheese" or "bread and meat," and one might hear peddlers calling out these phrases on busy London streets.

The first reference to a "sandwich" appears in the journal of Edward Gibbon, the English author and historian, in 1762. Gibbon observed it being eaten by a group of nobles and gentlemen in a fashionable London gaming club. It is no coincidence that this was the very gaming club frequented by a prominent aristocrat, politician, and frequent gamer of the same name as this nifty portable meal. Reportedly so engrossed in his gaming that he needed to eat with one hand while holding his cards with the other, John Montagu, the fourth Earl of Sandwich, is said to have ordered his favorite salt beef between two slices of bread at many occasions in the presence of other gentlemen; it seems likely that his peers requested "the same thing as Sandwich" enough times that the name caught on. However, it is a matter of ongoing contention among historians as to whether the Earl really did acquire his dining style while gaming as some assert or, as other historians suggest, at his desk during another period in his life, while consumed by his duties as Lord of the Admiralty during the American Revolution. A larger question for historians might be, with all that the Earl of Sandwich accomplished in his life, would he have

wanted his ticket to posterity tucked between two pieces of bread?

Regardless of origin, the sandwich became popular in the United States in the 1800s and made its first appearance in a cookbook in 1837, *Miss Leslie's Directions for Cookery*, which featured a ham sandwich, to be served on thinly sliced bread with a tarragon mustard. With the introduction of sliced bread in the early 1900s, and with the PR boost of cartoon husband Dagwood Bumstead and his impossibly tall sandwich creations, Americans began in earnest their ongoing love affair with the quick, easy, versatile, satisfying, sometimes prosaic and sometimes sublime sandwich.

grilled sausage
with smoked coleslaw

We surprised ourselves with how good this smoked coleslaw is. This is the vinegary kind of coleslaw, as opposed to one made with mayonnaise. We wanted some smoky flavor and didn't want to smoke the sausage, so we targeted the slaw instead, and a star was born. Whether you're adventurous in the kitchen or not, try this one. It's not hard to do, even without a smoker. Just set a rack inside an aluminum pan, and place wood chips beneath the rack (or tea leaves—they will burn readily and add a nice dimension to the smoked flavor). **MAKES 4 SANDWICHES**

½ small head savoy cabbage, cut in half and core removed

1 cup julienned carrots

½ cup thinly sliced red onion

¼ cup grapeseed oil

2 tablespoons white wine vinegar

1 teaspoon smoked or regular paprika

2 teaspoons Dijon mustard

½ teaspoon coriander seeds, crushed

¼ cup cilantro leaves, chopped

2 teaspoons kosher salt

½ serrano chile, finely chopped

4 sweet pork sausages

4 hero rolls, split

Use a large roasting pan with a rack at the bottom. Place a handful of wood chips, such as apple or cherry wood, or tea leaves, underneath the rack. Place the pan on a gas stove over high heat. Once the chips are smoking, separate the cabbage leaves and evenly distribute in the smoker. Close with a lid or cover tightly with aluminum foil. Smoke for about 15 minutes. When done, the cabbage will have a fairly smoky and slightly acidic flavor. Cut the cabbage into thin strips and add to a bowl with the carrots, onion, oil, vinegar, paprika, mustard, coriander, cilantro, salt, and chile. Mix into a slaw and set aside to marinate.

Grill the sausages whole on a grill or in a grill pan for about 15 minutes, until cooked through. (Or grill the sausages whole for a few minutes and then cut them in half and finish grilling on the cut side.)

Stuff the rolls with the cabbage slaw. Place the sausages on top, and follow with some more slaw. Serve immediately.

beer-braised beef short ribs with pickled vegetables, aged cheddar, and horseradish

1 teaspoon vegetable oil

1 pound boneless short ribs, cut into 4 pieces

½ small carrot, roughly chopped

½ small yellow onion, roughly chopped

2 garlic cloves, roughly chopped

2 cups brown ale

2 sprigs fresh rosemary

1 teaspoon kosher salt

½ teaspoon black peppercorns, roughly crushed

2 tablespoons prepared horseradish

1 baguette

4 thick slices aged Cheddar cheese

1 cup Pickled Vegetables (page 193)

Perennially popular at Craft are the short ribs braised in red wine. For our 'wichcraft sandwiches, though, we wanted something a bit different, so we chose to braise the short ribs in dark ale with horseradish. The light pickling of the vegetables is so quick there is no time for fermentation; the vegetables retain their crunch and acidity, which contrasts well with the richness of the meat. **MAKES 4 SANDWICHES**

Preheat the oven to 325°F.

Add the oil to a large, heavy-bottomed, ovenproof skillet over medium-high heat. Add the meat and sear until browned on all sides. Remove the meat from the skillet and set aside. Add the carrot, onion, and garlic to the same skillet and sauté until caramelized. Add the ale and deglaze. Place the meat back into the skillet and add the rosemary, salt, and pepper. Cover the skillet and transfer to the oven. Braise for about 2½ hours, until fork-tender. Remove and transfer the meat to a clean skillet. Keep oven on.

Strain the braising liquid and discard the fat. In a bowl, combine the strained liquid and the horseradish, and pour over the meat. Over low heat, glaze the meat as the liquid reduces. Remove from the heat when the pot is almost dry.

Cut the baguette into four pieces and slice each in half. Remove some of the bread from the top halves. Slice the meat and distribute one piece on each bottom half of bread. Spoon some of the liquids left in the skillet over the meat. Place the cheese on top of the meat and transfer to the oven together with the top slices of bread. Remove once the cheese is melted and the bread is toasted. Spread some horseradish on the top slices (optional). On the bottom halves, top the cheese with the pickled vegetables. Close the sandwiches, cut into halves, and serve.

party fare

You don't need us to tell you that sandwiches are a good fit for parties. Whether we're talking about an upscale party—after all, what's a canapé if not a beautiful one-bite sandwich—or Super Bowl Sunday, sandwiches are synonymous with celebration. This makes sense: portability is never more important in a meal than at a party, where people want to move about and socialize without juggling plate, knife, fork, and napkin in addition to a glass of beer or wine.

Sandwiches can be adapted to fit whatever mood you're hoping to strike. Many of the recipes in this book can be made as elegant canapés while others are perfect poolside. We think of three sandwich scenarios for a party: (1) the sandwiches made well in advance of the event; (2) the ingredients prepped well in advance and then assembled directly before the party begins; or (3) the guests assemble their own sandwiches during the party. Each of these scenarios carries its considerations.

If the sandwiches are made in advance

In many ways, prepping sandwiches in advance for a party is like prepping them for distribution in a restaurant. So the same rules apply:

- Be organized. If you're making three or four different kinds of sandwiches, plan out what needs to be prepped when. Then just follow your plan and execute one thing at a time.

- Think big. Do what the sandwich chefs do: make one large sandwich from a whole baguette and then cut that into individual servings. To make this work, wrap the whole loaf in parchment paper or waxed paper and then cut it into segments with a sharp bread knife.

- Twin the slices of bread. If you are using sliced bread to make individual sandwiches, remember that the end pieces are smaller than those in the middle, so take two from the same part of the loaf for each sandwich.

- Think "hardy." Even if you refrigerate the sandwiches for a while, there is a period of time—at the very least during the party—when they sit out without refrigeration. So it is important to select ingredients that can withstand this treatment. Steer clear of sandwiches with mayonnaise, for example, that will spoil, or chicken livers and the like, which will crust over and become unappetizing. Cured meats are safer in general than other preparations. Avoid ingredients that will wilt, dry out, or otherwise oxidize. Similarly, select a bread that will hold up over time.

- Cover your creations. Even the most resilient ingredients and breads need your help to endure. Once the sandwiches are assembled, do not leave them uncovered. Rather, place a very lightly damp paper towel atop the sandwiches. This will prevent the bread from getting dried out and crusty, and will keep the sandwiches from appearing and tasting as though they've been sitting around— even though they've been sitting around. Another way to "cover" your ingredients is to coat or top them. Let's say you're making a canapé with goat cheese and apple. Sliced ahead of time, the apple will turn brown. But if you think to soak the apple in simple syrup, you can keep the canapé looking and tasting lovely longer. If you absolutely have your heart set on a chopped chicken liver canapé or the like, you can keep it from crusting over as quickly by topping it with a little radish salad that will cover the liver and keep it both moist and cool.

- Don't stab your guests. Sounds silly, but people often use toothpicks to hold sandwiches together on party platters without realizing that the toothpicks are dangerous unless visible. Those little colored cellophane toppers aren't simply festive; they're there to alert guests and prevent harm from biting down on the sharp point of a toothpick. If you use toothpicks at all, please be sure they're easy to spot.

If the sandwiches will be made at the party, whether by or for the guests

- Keep the cooking and assembly areas separate. Raw foods tend to be unappetizing, and to further complicate matters, people who are preparing food while socializing tend to forget and use the same implements on both raw and cooked meats. Establish an area for sandwich assembly that is separate from the cooking space.

- Keep it all easy to assemble. Whether your guests will be making their own sandwiches or the sandwiches will be made for them, use fewer ingredients per sandwich and make them accessible and easy to work with. With hungry guests queuing up, the quicker the process (fun as it may be), the better. This applies to condiments as well. Giving your guests a choice adds to the interaction, but it should probably be a choice between two items, as opposed to among a whole array.

- Cover your bases. Offer a choice. If you're doing a panini party, for example, and one option is a pork roast, you may not also need a beef selection, but best to offer some sort of fish or chicken.

- Keep it simple. You may want a few exotic ingredients, but don't have all your choices be so uncommon that your guests feel inadequate or ignorant. They'll enjoy the experience more if they're familiar with most of the food.

How do you know how much food to buy? The short answer is, you don't. In running 'wichcraft, we have the benefit of seeing trends emerge. We come to know that we need to prep sixty chickens and forty beef. But unless you're throwing parties regularly, you don't have the benefit of experience to guide you. Most caterers and party planners recommend that you overbuy, making sure the leftovers are items you'll be happy to be stuck with. But how do you even calculate that? The general rule is to allot three to four ounces of meat (or chicken or fish) per person, unless you're serving a cured meat, in which case two ounces is plenty; an ounce and a half of cheese per person is ample as well. And know your audience. In New York City, the patrons at our financial district store are big meat eaters, while our Flatiron store gets many more salad orders and more adventurous palates generally. Time of year plays a role in people's food preferences, as well. Another consideration is the beverage choice you're offering: an emphasis on beer versus wine will incline guests toward different food selections.

If you're offering your guests the option of making their own sandwiches, you can do so around a theme. We've already mentioned the panini party, which is always fun. Please note that you do not need a panini press to host such a party: a heavy-bottomed pan placed atop the sandwich will press it just as well. Don't have one? Not to worry—take a heavy can of beans and put it on top of a regular pan to add the necessary weight. With proper supervision, kids really enjoy panini parties, at which they take grilled cheese in altogether new directions. Speaking of grilling cheeses, you could host a wine and cheese panini party, pairing great artisanal selections with wines that suit them. A *salumeria* (Italian name for a cured meat shop) theme might boast all cured meats (and again, nice wines). A greenmarket theme would work, with the day's offerings from local farms, whatever they might prove to be. And a winterfoods theme is always appreciated during the colder, darker months of the year.

But whatever you choose to do, please make it easy for your guests to meet and greet while eating. Guests have trouble socializing with a mouthful of bratwurst and onions. And they mingle less if their sandwiches are made on garlic bread. Parties necessarily place people in close proximity to one another, so please—be kind.

Now that everything's under control, go back to the party.

sweetsandwiches

chocolate cream'wich

FOR THE COOKIE

⅓ cup cocoa nibs

¾ cup (1½ sticks) unsalted butter, softened

⅔ cup dark brown sugar

⅔ cup granulated sugar

6 ounces bittersweet chocolate (64% cocoa), melted in a double boiler

1 tablespoon vanilla extract

1¾ cups all-purpose flour

1 teaspoon baking soda

½ teaspoon kosher salt

½ cup unsweetened cocoa powder

FOR THE FILLING

4 ounces bittersweet chocolate (64% cocoa), finely chopped

2 tablespoons unsalted butter

¼ teaspoon kosher salt

¼ cup heavy cream

Two surprises set this cookie apart: The first is that the filling is made with a chocolate ganache as opposed to just a frosting. The cream and the chocolate melt together perfectly, yielding a satisfyingly smooth texture to the filling itself. In contrast to the creaminess is the second surprise: the cocoa nibs, little pieces of roasted cacao beans. These bits add a crunchy texture that is wholly and delightfully unexpected.

MAKES 1 DOZEN SANDWICH COOKIES

Preheat the oven to 350°F.

TO MAKE THE COOKIES, grind the cocoa nibs in a coffee grinder or food processor until a fine powder. In the bowl of a stand mixer with the paddle attachment, combine the butter, ground cocoa nibs, and the sugars on medium speed until well mixed. Add the melted chocolate and the vanilla. Sift together the dry ingredients and add to the bowl. Mix into a smooth dough and chill in the freezer for 5 minutes.

Transfer the dough to a large surface covered with a layer of parchment paper. Top with another layer of parchment and gently roll the dough into a ¼-inch-thick sheet. To prevent the cookies from sticking as you cut them, carefully remove the top layer of parchment and sprinkle some flour over the sheet of dough. Replace the parchment, flip the dough, and release the parchment on the other side. Cut the dough into 2½-inch round cookies and space ½ inch apart on an ungreased cookie sheet. Gather any leftover scraps of dough and roll and cut as described above. Repeat until you have no dough left. Bake the cookies for about 15 minutes, turning the pan 90 degrees halfway through baking, until you can smell the toasted chocolate. Transfer the cookies to a cooling rack. Cool completely. Once cool, the cookies should be crisp.

TO MAKE THE FILLING, place the chocolate, butter, and salt in a medium mixing bowl. In a small saucepan, bring the cream to a boil and pour one-third of the cream over the chopped chocolate to melt the chocolate. Add the rest of the cream and stir until smooth. Let cool to room temperature.

Place half of the cookies with the top side (the most attractive) down. Using a piping bag or a spoon, evenly distribute the filling among those cookies, and close into sandwiches with the remaining cookies. Gently press down. Serve immediately or store the cookies in a cool place.

peanut butter cream'wich

FOR THE COOKIE

¾ cup (1½ sticks) unsalted butter

1 cup old-fashioned rolled oats

⅓ cup granulated sugar

½ cup dark brown sugar

½ cup creamy peanut butter

1 cup plus 2 tablespoons all-purpose flour

1 teaspoon baking soda

1 teaspoon kosher salt

FOR THE FILLING

4 tablespoons (½ stick) unsalted butter, softened

½ teaspoon salt

¼ cup confectioners' sugar

¾ cup creamy peanut butter

This is one of our most popular menu items. In fact, we receive numerous requests each year to have these shipped to folks across the country. Unfortunately, we are unable to do so because the cookies are so fragile. The secret ingredient in the cookie: oats. They add some texture and help keep the cookies together. **MAKES 1 DOZEN SANDWICH COOKIES**

Preheat the oven to 350°F.

TO MAKE THE COOKIES, melt 4 tablespoons of the butter in a saucepan over medium heat. Add the oats and cook, stirring frequently, for 5 to 7 minutes, until toasted. Pour the toasted oats onto a sheet pan and let cool. Combine the remaining ½ cup butter and the sugars in a stand mixer with the paddle attachment and mix until there are no chunks of butter left. Add the peanut butter and mix until combined. On low speed, add the toasted oats, then the flour, baking soda, and salt and blend into a smooth dough. Chill the dough in the freezer for 5 minutes.

Transfer the dough to a large surface covered with a layer of parchment paper. Top with another layer of parchment and gently roll the dough into a ¼-inch-thick sheet. To prevent the cookies from sticking as you cut them, carefully remove the top layer of parchment and sprinkle some flour over the sheet of dough. Replace the parchment, flip the dough, and release the parchment on the other side.

Cut the dough into 2½-inch round cookies and space about ½ inch apart on an ungreased cookie sheet. Gather any leftover scraps of dough and roll and cut as described above. Repeat until you have no dough left. Bake the cookies for about 20 minutes, turning the pan 90 degrees halfway through baking, until golden in color. Transfer the cookies to a cooling rack. Let cool completely before filling.

TO MAKE THE FILLING, combine the butter, salt, sugar, and peanut butter in the bowl of a stand mixer with the paddle attachment. Mix on medium speed until the filling is smooth.

Place half of the cookies with the top side (the most attractive) down. Using a piping bag or a spoon, evenly distribute the filling among those cookies, and close into sandwiches with the remaining cookies. Gently press down. Serve immediately or store the cookies in a cool place.

oatmeal cream'wich

FOR THE COOKIE

½ cup (1 stick) unsalted butter, softened

½ cup dark brown sugar

¼ cup granulated sugar

Grated zest of 1 lemon

½ teaspoon vanilla extract

1 egg, preferably pasture-raised

¾ cup all-purpose flour

½ teaspoon baking soda

⅛ teaspoon grated nutmeg

¼ teaspoon kosher salt

1½ cups old-fashioned rolled oats

FOR THE FILLING

2 tablespoons water

7 tablespoons granulated sugar

2 tablespoons heavy cream

5 tablespoons unsalted butter, softened

Pinch of kosher salt

¼ teaspoon vanilla extract

2 ounces cream cheese

The combination of the chewy cookie and the caramel–cream cheese filling has made this cookie many fans . . . so many, in fact, that though the cookie was originally introduced as a short-term special, our guests wouldn't permit us to remove it from the menu. But to enjoy it at home, please note that unlike the other two cream'wiches, this cookie does not last long once it has been filled with the cream. It will begin to grow soggy after about four hours. **MAKES ABOUT 1 DOZEN SANDWICH COOKIES**

Preheat the oven to 350°F.

TO MAKE THE COOKIES, combine the butter, sugars, lemon zest, and vanilla in the bowl of a stand mixer with the paddle attachment. Mix on medium speed until all ingredients come together and are light and fluffy. Add the egg. Sift together the flour, baking soda, nutmeg, and salt, and add to the butter mixture in three parts, waiting until each is well mixed before adding the next. Add the oats last, mixing just until combined. Chill the dough in the freezer for 5 minutes.

Transfer the dough to a large surface covered with a layer of parchment paper. Top with another layer of parchment and gently roll the dough into a ¼-inch-thick sheet. To prevent the cookies from sticking as you cut them, carefully remove the top layer of parchment and drizzle some flour over the sheet of dough. Replace the parchment, flip the dough, and release the parchment on the other side. Cut the dough into 2½-inch round cookies and space about ½ inch apart on an ungreased cookie sheet. Gather any leftover scraps of dough and roll and cut as described above. Repeat until you have no dough left. Bake the cookies for 15 to 20 minutes, turning the pan 90 degrees halfway through baking, until golden brown in color but still soft in the center. Transfer the cookies to a cooling rack. Let cool completely before filling.

TO MAKE THE FILLING, bring the water and 3 tablespoons of the sugar to a boil in a small heavy-bottomed saucepan. Once a dark brown color is achieved and the sugar looks like caramel, remove from the heat andd very carefully whisk in the cream. Allow to cool.

In the mixer with the paddle attachment, combine the butter with the remaining 4 tablespoons sugar and mix until the sugar is completely dissolved. Add the salt and vanilla, and once they are incorporated, turn the mixer down to a low speed and add the cream cheese and the caramel. Mix until fully incorporated.

Place half of the cookies with the top side (the most attractive) down. Using a piping bag or a spoon, evenly distribute the filling among those cookies, and close into sandwiches with the remaining cookies. Gently press down. Serve immediately or store the cookies in a cool place.

banana bread with caramel ice cream and pecan brittle

Here, the brittle adds the excitement to the ice cream sandwich by providing the crunch. But don't add the brittle too far in advance, as it will begin to dissolve into the ice cream. If pecans are not your favorite, you can substitute a nut that's more to your liking. **MAKES 4 ICE CREAM SANDWICHES**

Preheat the oven to 350°F. Brush a 9 x 5-inch loaf pan with butter and line the bottom of the pan with parchment paper.

TO MAKE THE BANANA BREAD, whisk together the sugar and oil in a medium bowl. Add the bananas, eggs, sour cream, and vanilla and whisk together until smooth. Sift the flour, baking soda, and salt into the banana mixture. Using a rubber spatula, fold the dry ingredients into the wet ingredients until just combined. Pour the batter into the prepared pan and set on a baking sheet. Bake for 50 minutes to 1 hour, rotating the pan 90 degrees after 30 minutes, until golden and firm to the touch and a cake tester inserted in the center comes out clean. Remove the cake from the oven, let rest in the pan for 5 minutes, then remove from the pan and transfer to a cooling rack.

TO MAKE THE ICE CREAM, place 1¼ cups of the sugar in a large saucepan with about 1 tablespoon of water; it should look like damp sand. Cook over high heat until the sugar melts and becomes a very dark, smoking caramel. Remove the pan from the heat and very carefully whisk in the cream and then the milk. Return the pan to the heat and bring the liquid to a rolling boil. Whisk together the egg yolks and the remaining ¼ cup sugar. Temper the yolks by gradually whisking about half of the hot cream into the yolks and then returning it all to the pan and whisking it together. Add the salt and the vanilla. Strain through a fine-mesh sieve. Chill this mixture over ice and transfer to an ice cream maker. Process according to the manufacturer's instructions. Transfer the ice cream to a covered container and place in the freezer for about 2 hours, until firm.

RECIPE CONTINUES

FOR THE BANANA BREAD

1½ cups sugar

¾ cup grapeseed oil

¾ cup banana puree (1½ medium bananas, pureed until smooth in a blender)

¾ cup mashed bananas (1½ medium bananas, mashed with a fork)

3 large eggs, preferably pasture-raised

¾ cup sour cream

1½ teaspoons vanilla extract

2¼ cups all-purpose flour

1½ teaspoons baking soda

¾ teaspoon kosher salt

FOR THE ICE CREAM

1½ cups sugar

1 tablespoon water

2 cups heavy cream

2 cups milk

9 large egg yolks, preferably pasture-raised

¾ teaspoon kosher salt

½ teaspoon vanilla extract

FOR THE PECAN BRITTLE

1½ cups shelled pecans

1 cup sugar

¼ cup water

4 tablespoons (½ stick) unsalted butter

6 tablespoons light corn syrup

¼ teaspoon baking soda

¼ teaspoon kosher salt

Sea salt

Preheat the oven to 350°F and butter a sheet pan.

TO MAKE THE PECAN BRITTLE, spread the pecans on a baking sheet and toast in the oven until they are fragrant and dark brown. In a 4-quart pot, mix the sugar, water, butter, and corn syrup and bring to a boil. Cook over high heat, stirring occasionally to avoid sticking to the bottom, until a light caramel color (or, if using a candy thermometer, until it reaches 300°F). Remove from the heat and very carefully stir in the baking soda, pecans, and salt. Working very quickly before it cools, spread the mixture over the buttered sheet pan using a heat-resistant rubber spatula. Once it is completely cooled, break into small pieces.

When ready to assemble, let the ice cream defrost at room temperature for 15 minutes. Mix the brittle into the softened ice cream. Evenly spread the ice cream over 4 (½-inch-thick) slices of banana bread, covering them all the way to the edge. (The ice cream must be soft enough to avoid ripping the bread.) Sprinkle some sea salt over the ice cream, close the sandwiches with a matching 4 slices of banana bread, and place in the freezer for at least 1 hour before serving.

sweets for the sweet

On August 19, 1900, the *New York Telegraph* ran the following item, which was reprinted in the *Washington Post*: "The ice cream sandwich is a new hot weather luxury which is rapidly coming into downtown favor. An enterprising hokeypokey vendor, whose daily station is in John Street, is the projector, and his push cart is constantly surrounded by a jostling, sweltering crowd of patrons, representing all social conditions, from banker down to bootblack and newsboy. The inventor takes a graham wafer, deftly plasters it with ice cream, claps another wafer on top, and there is your ice cream sandwich. The cost is trifling, ranging from 2 to 3 cents, according to the size and thickness of the thing. But the man is simply coining money, where he eked out a meager revenue before. He has simply tickled the public's fancy for something new."

Less seasonal than ice cream bars or cones, the ice cream sandwich has since become a top-selling form of ice cream. And the classic sandwich cookie—two chocolate wafers with vanilla cream between them—was the largest-selling cookie of the twentieth century and remains in the lead in the twenty-first, reaching over 490 billion to date. So it seems that portability, great flavor, and the fun factor of a sandwich are attributes every bit as winning in a sweet snack as they are in a quick meal.

We thought we would feature some ice cream sandwiches at 'wichcraft. Karen DeMasco, the former pastry chef at Craft, was excited about the project and volunteered to help develop a handful of recipes (literally, a handful). She came up with a great selection that, while not all actual sandwiches, were portable and easy to eat with one's hands. The most popular sweet item at 'wichcraft is the Peanut Butter Cream'wich (page 160). Once the recipes had been perfected, Karen put Erica Leahy in charge of baking them every day at the Craft kitchen. When we got our own kitchen in West Chelsea, Erica became 'wichcraft's pastry chef, continuing to make our classic cream'wiches and adding her own creations over time.

Karen and Erica had great fun playing with the concepts of the sandwich cookie and so can you. The same principles apply to sweet sandwiches as to savory: think architecture to ensure portability and strive for balanced flavors and textures. For example, if the inside is very sweet, the outside probably shouldn't be, and vice versa. Flavors you already enjoy together are natural choices, such as hazelnut with chocolate and banana, peanut butter and chocolate, or dried fruit and nuts. And, while it might be fun to experiment with gingerbread, or zucchini or banana bread, be sure that the exterior is firm enough not to fall apart. Also, holiday times are great times for branching out: next December, Sisha wants to try a sandwich of fruitcake with eggnog ice cream and another using panettone.

gingerbread with rum ice cream and poached pears

FOR THE POACHED PEARS

⅔ cup granulated sugar

⅔ cup cider vinegar

⅔ cup water

1 star anise

1 teaspoon black peppercorns

2 whole cloves

Pinch of ground peperoncino or red pepper flakes

½ cinnamon stick

2 Bartlett pears, peeled, cored, and cut into ⅛-inch slices

FOR THE GINGERBREAD

¾ cup dark stout beer, such as Guinness

6 tablespoons brewed coffee

¾ cup molasses

¾ teaspoon baking soda

1 cup dark brown sugar

7 tablespoons grapeseed oil

4 tablespoons sugar in the raw

2 tablespoons grated fresh ginger

1 large egg, preferably pasture-raised

1¾ cups plus 2 tablespoons all-purpose flour

2¼ teaspoons baking powder

2¼ teaspoons ground ginger

2¼ teaspoons unsweetened cocoa powder

We used pears in this ice cream'wich, but many other fruits would work well, too, such as apples, figs, or peaches. Because the fruit is poached, it won't harden in the same way that raw fruit does when it is frozen. And not to worry if you do not like rum: you can simply leave it out of the ice cream recipe, yielding a simple and tasty vanilla ice cream. **MAKES 4 ICE CREAM SANDWICHES**

TO MAKE THE POACHED PEARS, in a saucepan, combine the sugar, vinegar, water, star anise, peppercorns, cloves, peperoncino, and cinnamon stick, and bring to a boil. Reduce the heat and simmer for 15 minutes. Add the pears, bring it back to a simmer, and cook for 2 to 3 minutes, until tender. Remove from the heat and cool in the liquid. Unless used right away, transfer the pears and liquid to a container. (Keeps in the refrigerator for 1 to 2 weeks.)

Preheat oven to 350°F. Butter a 9 x 5-inch loaf pan and line the bottom with parchment paper.

TO MAKE THE GINGERBREAD, bring the beer, coffee, and molasses to a boil in a medium saucepan. Remove from the heat and whisk in the baking soda. Transfer the mixture to a small bowl and place the bowl into a larger bowl filled with ice water. Stir until mixture is cool and set aside.

In a bowl, whisk together the brown sugar, oil, 3 tablespoons of the sugar in the raw, and fresh ginger. Whisk in the egg. In a large bowl, sift together the flour, baking powder, ground ginger, cocoa powder, cinnamon, salt, nutmeg, and pepper. In three parts, alternate adding the wet ingredients and the dry ingredients to the brown sugar mixture, whisking to combine. Pour the batter into the prepared pan and sprinkle the remaining tablespoon of sugar in the raw on top. Bake for about 45 minutes to 1 hour, until the loaf is golden and a toothpick inserted into the center comes out clean. Do not open the

RECIPE CONTINUES

1½ teaspoons ground
cinnamon

½ teaspoon kosher salt

⅛ teaspoon grated nutmeg

⅛ teaspoon ground
white pepper

FOR THE RUM ICE CREAM

2 vanilla beans

1¼ cups granulated sugar

2 cups milk

2 cups heavy cream

9 egg yolks, preferably
pasture-raised

¾ teaspoon kosher salt

⅓ cup dark rum, such as
Myers's

Freshly ground black pepper

oven frequently during baking; wait until the gingerbread has cooked for 40 minutes, then turn the pan 90 degrees. Remove from the oven, let rest in the pan for 5 minutes, then remove from the pan and transfer to a cooling rack.

TO MAKE THE ICE CREAM, split the vanilla beans lengthwise and scrape the seeds from each side into the measured sugar. In a medium saucepan, combine the milk, cream, and half of the vanilla sugar. Whisk together and bring to a full rolling boil over medium-high heat. While the milk mixture is heating, whisk together the egg yolks and the remaining vanilla sugar. Temper the eggs into the boiling milk mixture by removing the saucepan from the heat and pouring half of it over the yolks. Whisk well and return the yolk mixture to the saucepan. Whisk in the salt. In a metal bowl over ice, chill the ice cream base thoroughly. Strain the base through a fine-mesh sieve. Whisk the rum into the ice cream base. Process the base in an ice cream maker according to the manufacturer's instructions. Transfer the ice cream to a covered container and place in the freezer for about 2 hours, until it is firm.

When ready to assemble, let the ice cream defrost at room temperature for 15 minutes. Evenly spread the softened ice cream over 4 (½-inch-thick) slices of gingerbread, covering them all the way to the edge. (The ice cream must be soft enough to avoid ripping the bread.) Top the ice cream with the pear slices and season with pepper. Close the sandwiches with a matching 4 slices of gingerbread and place in the freezer for at least 1 hour before serving.

devil's food cake with vanilla ice cream and sour cherries

The classic combination of chocolate cake, cherries, and cream found in the traditional Black Forest cake was our inspiration for this cream'wich. In the summertime, fresh cherries can be used in lieu of dried. As is true of all of our ice cream sandwiches, we advise that you make them at least a short while in advance of when you want to serve them. Otherwise, the ice cream tends to squeeze out the sides. **MAKES 4 ICE CREAM SANDWICHES**

Preheat the oven to 350°F. Butter a 9 x 5-inch loaf pan and line the bottom with parchment paper.

TO MAKE THE DEVIL'S FOOD CAKE, whisk together the cocoa and water in a bowl to make a paste. Sift together the flours, baking powder, baking soda, and salt. In the bowl of a stand mixer with the paddle attachment, combine the butter, brown sugar, and vanilla on medium speed. Add the egg and the yolk, followed by the cocoa paste. Once combined, alternate adding the dry ingredients and the buttermilk. Pour the batter into the prepared pan and bake for 45 minutes to 1 hour, turning after the first 30 minutes, until the cake is firm to the touch and a knife inserted into the center comes out clean. Remove the cake from the oven, let rest in the pan for 5 minutes, then remove from the pan and transfer to a cooling rack.

TO MAKE THE ICE CREAM, split the vanilla beans lengthwise and scrape the seeds from each side into the measured sugar. In a medium saucepan, combine the milk, cream, and half of the vanilla sugar. Whisk together and bring to a full rolling boil over medium-high heat. While the milk mixture is heating, whisk together the egg yolks and the remaining vanilla sugar. Temper the eggs into the boiling milk mixture by removing the saucepan from the heat and pouring half of it over the yolks. Whisk this well and return the yolk mixture to the saucepan. Whisk in the salt. In a metal bowl over ice, chill

RECIPE CONTINUES

FOR THE DEVIL'S FOOD CAKE

¾ cup unsweetened cocoa powder, such as Valrhona

½ cup plus 1 tablespoon warm water

¾ cup cake flour

¾ cup all-purpose flour

½ teaspoon baking powder

¾ teaspoon baking soda

½ teaspoon kosher salt

5 tablespoons unsalted butter, softened

1¾ cups dark brown sugar

¾ teaspoon vanilla extract

1 egg, plus 1 yolk, preferably pasture-raised

½ cup plus 2 tablespoons buttermilk

FOR THE ICE CREAM

2 vanilla beans

1¼ cups granulated sugar

2 cups milk

2 cups heavy cream

9 egg yolks, preferably pasture-raised

¾ teaspoon kosher salt

the ice cream base thoroughly. Strain the base through a fine-mesh sieve. Process the base in an ice cream maker according to the manufacturer's instructions. Transfer the ice cream to a covered container and place in the freezer until it is firm, about 2 hours.

TO MAKE THE SOUR CHERRIES, in a small pot, combine the wine, sugar, and anise seeds and heat until the sugar is dissolved. Add the dried cherries, stir, and slowly reduce the mixture until it has the consistency of a syrup. Set aside to cool. When ready to assemble, let the ice cream defrost at room temperature for 15 minutes. Mix the sour cherries into the ice cream.

Evenly spread the ice cream over 4 (½-inch-thick) slices of the chocolate cake, covering them all the way to the edge. (The ice cream must be soft enough to avoid ripping the bread.) Top with a matching 4 slices of chocolate cake and place them in the freezer for at least 1 hour before serving.

FOR THE SOUR CHERRIES
¼ cup red wine or port
¼ cup granulated sugar
½ teaspoon anise seeds
½ cup dried sour cherries

pantry

,,,,,

mayonnaise

1 large egg yolk, preferably from a pasture-raised egg

½ teaspoon Dijon mustard

½ teaspoon chopped garlic

Pinch of cayenne pepper

1 tablespoon white wine vinegar

1 cup grapeseed oil

¼ cup extra-virgin olive oil

½ teaspoon kosher salt

Freshly ground black pepper

MAKES ABOUT 1½ CUPS

Place the egg yolk, mustard, garlic, cayenne pepper, and vinegar in a food processor or blender. Start the blender and slowly add the grapeseed oil in a thin, even stream. When half of the oil has been added, add 1 tablespoon water. Then slowly add the remaining grapeseed oil and blend until fully incorporated. If the mayonnaise looks a bit thick, add another 1 teaspoon of water. Slowly add the olive oil and blend until you have a smooth mayonnaise (see Note). Season with the salt and pepper. Use immediately or store in the refrigerator for 2 to 3 days.

NOTE This recipe uses raw eggs, which should not be served to pregnant women, young children, the elderly, or anyone whose health is compromised. Pasteurized eggs may be substituted.

black chile mayonnaise

MAKES ABOUT 1½ CUPS

Place an oven or cooling rack on top of a gas burner. Make sure you're cooking in a well-ventilated area to avoid breathing in the fumes that will generate when charring the chiles (see Note). Place the chiles on the rack and char over an open flame. (You can also char the chiles in a cast-iron skillet over high heat.) Using tongs, turn the chiles as they char. The chiles will puff up and turn completely black. Remove from the heat and cool.

Discard the stems from all the chiles as well as the seeds from the ancho. Transfer the chiles to a blender or food processor and grind until fine. Place in a bowl and combine with the oil.

In a food processor, combine the egg yolk, garlic, lime juice, sugar, salt, and 2 tablespoons water, and quickly blend. With the food processor at medium to low speed, slowly add the chile oil in a thin and steady stream until fully incorporated. If some of the chile mix sticks to the side of the bowl, stop the blender and use a spatula to fully incorporate and blend together until smooth (see Note). Use immediately or store in the refrigerator for 2 to 3 days.

NOTE Don't underestimate the need for proper ventilation. The fumes of the chiles can be extremely powerful.

If the mayonnaise starts looking thick at any point and sticks to the side of the machine, add just a drizzle of water until you have a desired consistency. Depending on the size and shape of your blender, you may need to use a spatula to scoop up all the ingredients and ensure that they get fully incorporated.

This recipe uses raw eggs, which should not be served to pregnant women, young children, the elderly, or anyone whose health is compromised. Pasteurized eggs may be substituted.

2 chipotle chiles

1 ancho chile

1 cup grapeseed oil

1 large egg yolk, preferably from a pasture-raised egg

½ teaspoon minced garlic

Juice from 1 lime

¼ teaspoon sugar

½ teaspoon kosher salt

black olive mayonnaise

1 large egg yolk, preferably from a pasture-raised egg

½ teaspoon Dijon mustard

½ teaspoon chopped garlic

2 tablespoons pitted and chopped Niçoise olives

1 tablespoon white wine vinegar

½ cup extra-virgin olive oil

¼ cup grapeseed oil

Freshly ground black pepper

MAKES ABOUT 1 CUP

Place the egg yolk, mustard, garlic, olives, and vinegar in a food processor or blender. Start the blender and add 1 tablespoon water. With the blender running evenly at medium to low speed, slowly add the olive oil in a thin, even stream. Then add the grapeseed oil, season with the pepper, and blend until you have a smooth mayonnaise (see Note). Use immediately or store in a tightly covered container in the refrigerator for 2 to 3 days.

NOTE This recipe uses raw eggs, which should not be served to pregnant women, young children, the elderly, or anyone whose health is compromised. Pasteurized eggs may be substituted.

lemon mayonnaise

1 large egg yolk, preferably from a pasture-raised egg

½ teaspoon Dijon mustard

½ teaspoon chopped garlic

Pinch of cayenne pepper

4 teaspoons lemon juice

1 cup grapeseed oil

¼ cup oil from Lemon Confit (see page 200), or ¼ cup extra-virgin olive oil plus grated zest from 1 lemon

½ teaspoon kosher salt

Freshly ground black pepper

MAKES ABOUT 1½ CUPS

Place the egg yolk, mustard, garlic, cayenne pepper, and the lemon juice in a food processor or blender. Add the lemon zest, if using. Start the blender and slowly start adding the grapeseed oil in a thin, even stream. When about half of the oil has been added, add 1 tablespoon water. Then slowly add the remaining grapeseed oil and blend until fully incorporated. If the mayonnaise looks a bit thick at this point, add a drizzle of water. Slowly add the lemon oil (or olive oil), season with the salt and pepper, and blend until you have a smooth mayonnaise (see Note). Use immediately or store in the refrigerator for 2 to 3 days.

NOTE This recipe uses raw eggs, which should not be served to pregnant women, young children, the elderly, or anyone whose health is compromised. Pasteurized eggs may be substituted.

lemon vinaigrette

1 cup extra-virgin olive oil

⅔ cup fresh lemon juice

2 tablespoons finely chopped shallots

2 teaspoons kosher salt

1 sprig fresh rosemary

MAKES ABOUT 2 CUPS

In a bowl, combine the oil, lemon juice, shallots, and salt and whisk until the vinaigrette emulsifies. Add the rosemary sprig, cover, and set aside for 1 hour. Remove the rosemary before using. Keeps well if refrigerated for up to 1 week.

parsley vinaigrette

2 tablespoons finely chopped shallots

1 teaspoon chopped capers

1 tablespoon extra-virgin olive oil

1 tablespoon white wine

2 teaspoons white wine vinegar

¼ teaspoon kosher salt

¼ cup picked flat-leaf parsley leaves

MAKES ABOUT ½ CUP

In a bowl, combine all the ingredients and mix well. Keeps well if refrigerated for up to 3 or 4 days.

pistachio vinaigrette

MAKES ABOUT ¾ CUP

Preheat the oven to 350°F.

Pour the pistachios onto a sheet pan and toast in the oven for 5 to 10 minutes. Remove and transfer 4 tablespoons of pistachios to a blender or food processor. Add the oil, vinegar, ½ cup water, parsley, salt, and pepper to taste, and blend the vinaigrette until smooth. Finely chop the remaining 1 tablespoon pistachios and add to the vinaigrette. Keeps well if refrigerated for up to 3 to 4 days.

5 tablespoons roasted unsalted pistachio nuts

¼ cup extra-virgin olive oil

2 tablespoons white wine vinegar

1 tablespoon chopped flat-leaf parsley

½ teaspoon kosher salt

Freshly ground black pepper

hazelnut brown butter

MAKES ABOUT ½ CUP

In a skillet over medium-high heat, toast the hazelnuts until deep brown in color, about 3 to 5 minutes. Remove from the skillet, finely chop, and return to the skillet. Add the anise seeds and allow them to toast for a few seconds, constantly shaking the pan to avoid burning. Add the butter and sage, and stir constantly. Season with the salt and pepper and continue to stir until the butter has a nutty brown color. Transfer the butter to a container, remove the sage leaves, and refrigerate. Once the butter has cooled, stir again to ensure that all the ingredients are evenly mixed. Use immediately or store in the refrigerator for 2 to 4 weeks.

4 tablespoons shelled hazelnuts

½ teaspoon anise seeds

3 tablespoons unsalted butter

4 sage leaves

¼ teaspoon kosher salt

Freshly ground black pepper

roasted onions

4 tablespoons extra-virgin olive oil

4 medium yellow onions, halved and cut lengthwise into ⅛-inch slices

2 tablespoons chopped fresh oregano, or 1 tablespoon dried Sicilian oregano

Kosher salt and freshly ground black pepper

MAKES 2 CUPS

In a skillet over medium-high heat, add the olive oil and onions and stir vigorously to avoid scorching. Add the oregano and season with salt and pepper. Continue stirring until the onions have a deep brown color. Reduce the heat and continue to cook until the onions are soft, 30 to 45 minutes. Use immediately or refrigerate for up to 1 week.

tomato relish

2 tablespoons extra-virgin olive oil

1 small yellow onion, halved and thinly sliced lengthwise

1 garlic clove, finely chopped

1 tablespoon sugar

1 teaspoon curry powder

1 tablespoon sherry vinegar

1 (28-ounce) can whole tomatoes

2 teaspoons chopped fresh oregano, or 1 teaspoon dried Sicilian oregano

2 teaspoons kosher salt

Freshly ground black pepper

¼ cup flat-leaf parsley leaves, chopped

2 tablespoons drained Pickled Mustard Seeds (see page 187)

MAKES 1¼ CUPS

Pour the olive oil into a skillet over medium-high heat. Add the onion and garlic and sauté until they are golden brown. Add the sugar and curry powder and cook for 5 minutes. Add the vinegar and deglaze the pan. Add the tomatoes, oregano, salt, and pepper to taste and simmer for 30 minutes. Remove from the heat and pour the contents into a strainer. Stir the relish so most of the liquid drains (see Note). Transfer to a cutting board and roughly chop. Transfer to a bowl and mix in the parsley and mustard seeds. Check the seasoning and adjust if necessary. Use immediately or store refrigerated for up to 1 week.

NOTE Consider reserving the liquid from the relish to reheat any leftover meatloaf or other meats. It's also great as the base of a flavorful tomato sauce or dressing.

roasted peppers

2 red bell peppers

1 teaspoon chopped garlic

1 teaspoon chopped fresh rosemary

8 basil leaves

2 tablespoons extra-virgin olive oil

Kosher salt and freshly ground black pepper

MAKES 1 TO 1½ CUPS

Char the peppers over an open flame (on the stove or a grill) until the skin is black but not brittle. Make sure to use as high a heat as possible. The skin should char without the peppers cooking for too long. Transfer the peppers to a bowl and cover with plastic wrap. The steam will help to loosen the skin. Once they are slightly cool, remove all the skin, seeds, and stems. The skin should come off easily. (Do not submerge the peppers in water as this would wash away the flavor. A little of the charred skin left on them is fine.) Slice the peppers lengthwise into strips about ¼ inch wide. In a bowl, mix the peppers with the garlic, rosemary, basil, and oil. Season well with salt and pepper. Use immediately or refrigerate for up to 1 week.

black chile oil

MAKES ABOUT 1¼ CUPS

Place an oven or cooling rack on top of a gas burner. Make sure you're cooking in a well-ventilated area to avoid breathing in the fumes that will generate when charring the chiles (see Note, page 177). Place the chiles on the rack and char over an open flame. (You can also char the chiles in a cast-iron skillet over high heat.) Using tongs, turn the chiles as they char. The chiles will puff up and turn completely black. Remove from the heat and cool.

Discard the stems from all the chiles as well as the seeds from the anchos. Add the chiles and all the remaining ingredients to a food processor or blender and mix until fully incorporated. Use immediately or transfer to a container and refrigerate for 2 to 4 weeks.

8 dried chipotle chiles

2 dried ancho chiles

¾ cup grapeseed oil

2 tablespoons white wine vinegar

2 tablespoons sugar

1 tablespoon minced garlic

1 tablespoon kosher salt

Juice from ½ lime

pickled mustard seeds

MAKES 2 CUPS

In a saucepan, bring 1 cup water, vinegar, sugar, and mustard to a boil. Add the mustard seeds and simmer for 5 minutes, until the seeds bloom (double in size). Remove from the heat and cool. Store the mustard seeds in the liquid. Keeps well if refrigerated for up to 2 weeks.

1 cup white wine vinegar

1 cup sugar

1 tablespoon dry mustard

½ cup mustard seeds

pickled pepper relish

MAKES ABOUT 1 CUP

Drain the peppers and remove the stems. Combine with the vinegar and sugar in a food processor or blender and blend until finely chopped. Depending on the peppers you use, you may need to adjust the amounts of vinegar and/or sugar. Add a little vinegar and sugar at a time, and taste the relish as you go. The flavors should be balanced and not too sweet or tangy. Keeps well if refrigerated for up to 1 week.

2 cups jarred hot pickled peppers, such as Italian cherry peppers or peppadews

2 tablespoons white wine vinegar

2 teaspoons sugar

pantry provisions

A well-stocked pantry is essential for anyone who loves to cook, largely because it grants freedom; you can stroll the greenmarket or stop in at the butcher for just the starring elements of a meal, knowing that the supporting players are already at home.

Pantry items are usually condiments—items with assertive, often layered flavors that will complement the meal's principal ingredients, whether by accentuating them or by mellowing them. You know instinctively how to match pantry items with the main elements of a meal. Rich, fatty meats benefit from some acid or spice to cut them. Lean turkey or chicken breasts profit from some added richness, such as mayonnaise. And even in those cases wherein two rich items are paired—bacon and eggs, for example—one is generally mellow, like the egg, while the other is assertive, like the bacon. Much of what you have always done already intuitively reflects this balancing act: Mustard adds spice, sweetness, and acidity that balances a rich hot dog. Lemon highlights the freshness of a fish fillet. Peanut butter is rich and salty—the bass notes of the PBJ sandwich—while jelly adds the sweet, tart high notes that harmonize well with them. Though which ingredient is the condiment in that sandwich is certainly up for debate.

Lemon Confit (page 200) is a great all-around condiment, as it covers the spectrum of flavors: sourness from the lemon; sweetness and salt because of its cure; bitterness from the rind, and added garlic. Interestingly, a whole meal can be inspired by and spring up around a pantry item—a relish or marmalade or confit that fairly calls to us to poach a particular fish or braise a certain cut of meat to pair with it. And sometimes what began as a condiment soon becomes worthy of main-ingredient status, with the accompanying meat now the condiment in the equation.

Keep certain basics always on hand. These can be purchased ahead and stored in your pantry or refrigerator for later use. The exception to this is butter; it absorbs the flavors of your fridge, so don't buy too much of it ahead of time, and keep it well wrapped. You can also keep it in the freezer until you need it.

Pantry Staples

- Extra-virgin olive oil. Buy the best you can afford because it's worth it.
- A selection of high-quality vinegars, including red wine vinegar, sherry vinegar, and a nicely aged balsamic. Make sure the label reads "balsamic vinegar." If it reads "balsamic condiment" it's not the real thing.
- Sea salt, coarse or flakes
- Kosher salt
- Black peppercorns and a good grinder
- Dijon mustard and a grainier mustard like Moutarde de Meaux
- Anchovies packed in olive oil or anchovy paste
- Preserved hot peppers, as a paste, pickled, or in sauce form
- Prepared grated horseradish
- Capers, nonpareil, in brine
- Assorted spices and seeds—coriander, cumin, fennel seeds
- Dried chiles
- Dried oregano, tarragon, and herbes de Provence
- Garlic and onions

Refrigerator Staples

- Good-quality unsalted butter
- Assorted olives
- Pickles—cornichons, peppers, green beans, etc.
- Fruit preserves
- Good bread, keeps in the freezer for up to 2 months.
- Lemons

In general, when a pantry item can be made rather than purchased, and you have the time, we encourage you to do so. The ingredients will be fresher, there will be fewer preservatives and additives, and the taste or texture (and sometimes both) is bound to be better. A great example is the roasted red pepper. Jarred or canned, roasted red peppers are usually made in large batches by machine and tend to be overcooked, with a texture that can only be described as "smooshy." With very little effort, though, you can make these very well yourself (page 184).

Of course, there are times when you should save your energy. Making sauerkraut, for example, requires a great deal of room, takes months to complete, and creates a terrible odor, yielding an end product that will probably not be as good as something you could have purchased inexpensively at the supermarket.

But this certainly does not apply to the recipes on these pages. We welcome hearing about the meals—portable or otherwise—that they inspire you to create.

pickled red onions

1¼ cups red wine vinegar

¼ cup sugar

1 teaspoon curry powder

1 teaspoon black peppercorns

1 teaspoon fennel seeds

1 teaspoon coriander seeds

2 small red onions, sliced

MAKES ABOUT 3 CUPS

In a saucepan, combine the vinegar, ½ cup water, sugar, and spices and bring to a boil. Remove from the heat, add the onions, and stir. Set aside to cool, stirring occasionally. Keeps well if refrigerated for up to 2 to 3 weeks.

grilled red onions

1 medium red onion, sliced crosswise into ¼-inch wheels

4 teaspoons extra-virgin olive oil

½ teaspoon finely chopped fresh rosemary

¼ teaspoon curry powder

1 teaspoon Worcestershire sauce

¼ teaspoon kosher salt

Freshly ground black pepper

MAKES ABOUT 1 CUP

Brush the wheels of onion with 3 teaspoons of the oil. In a grill pan or cast-iron skillet over high heat, grill the onions (without separating into individual rings) until charred on the outside and slightly cooked on the inside. Place them in a bowl and separate into rings. Add the remaining teaspoon of oil and season with the rosemary, curry, Worcestershire sauce, salt, and pepper. Use immediately or store in the refrigerator for up to 1 week.

pickled vegetables

MAKES ABOUT 3 CUPS (DRAINED VEGETABLES)

In a saucepan, combine 2 cups water, the vinegar, wine, sugar, fennel seeds, coriander seeds, peppercorns, star anise, and salt and bring to a boil. Remove from the heat, and pour into a large bowl containing the fennel, carrot, radishes, and garlic. Set aside and refrigerate for at least 24 hours. Keeps well if refrigerated in its liquid for up to 2 weeks.

1 cup white wine vinegar

1 cup white wine

½ cup sugar

1 teaspoon fennel seeds

1 teaspoon coriander seeds

1 teaspoon black peppercorns

5 star anise

1 teaspoon kosher salt

½ bulb fennel, halved lengthwise and sliced (about 1 cup)

½ large carrot, sliced on the bias and cut in half (about 1 cup)

1 cup thinly sliced radishes

4 garlic cloves

balsamic onion marmalade

MAKES 2 TO 3 CUPS

Heat the oil in a large skillet over medium heat until it slides easily across the pan. Add the onions, salt, and pepper and cook, stirring occasionally, for about 20 minutes, until the onions are soft. Add the sugar and reduce the heat to medium-low. Cook, stirring frequently, for about 10 minutes, until the onions appear dry. Add the vinegar and reduce the heat to low. Continue cooking, stirring occasionally, for about 1 hour, until the onions are soft and dry. Serve warm or at room temperature. Store the marmalade in the refrigerator. It will keep for several weeks.

1 tablespoon vegetable oil

4 medium onions, thinly sliced (about 8 cups)

Kosher salt and freshly ground black pepper

⅓ cup sugar

⅔ cup balsamic vinegar

raisin-pinenut relish

¼ cup pinenuts

3 tablespoons extra-virgin olive oil

½ cup diced yellow onion

1 teaspoon finely chopped garlic

½ cup dark raisins

½ cup white wine vinegar

½ cup Roasted Peppers (page 184), roughly chopped

4 fillets salt-cured anchovies, finely chopped

2 teaspoons chopped fresh oregano, or 1 teaspoon dried Sicilian oregano

MAKES ABOUT 1½ CUPS

Lightly toast the pinenuts in a skillet over medium-high heat. Be careful to not toast them too much as they will take on a bitter flavor. Set aside.

Pour the oil into the hot skillet. Add the onion and sauté over medium-high heat until golden, stirring occasionally. Add the garlic and sauté for another minute or so until the garlic is fragrant. Add the raisins and the vinegar. Reduce the heat and continue cooking for 2 to 3 minutes, until the vinegar has reduced by half and the raisins are plump. Add the peppers, followed by the anchovies, ½ cup water, and pinenuts. Stir and reduce the heat to low. Cover the skillet with a lid and cook for another 10 minutes, until most of the water has evaporated. Once the relish has dried, add the oregano and stir well. Allow to cool completely before using. Keeps well if refrigerated for up to 1 week.

roasted tomatoes

MAKES 40 TOMATO HALVES

Preheat the oven to 350°F.

Cut the tomatoes in half crosswise (through the equator), then place the tomatoes, garlic, and oil in a large bowl. Season with salt and pepper and mix gently. Line two large, rimmed sheet pans with parchment paper or aluminum foil. Place the tomato halves on the sheet pans cut side down, and then pour over them any oil left in the bowl. Divide the garlic and thyme between the sheet pans and bake for about 20 minutes, until the tomato skins loosen. Remove and discard the tomato skins. Pour any juices that may have accumulated into a bowl and reserve.

Return the tomatoes to the oven and reduce the temperature to 275°F. Continue roasting, periodically pouring off and reserving any juices, for 3 to 4 hours more, until the tomatoes are slightly shrunken and appear cooked and concentrated but not yet dry. Remove the tomatoes from the oven and allow them to cool on the sheet pans. Discard the thyme sprigs and the garlic. Transfer the tomatoes to a container. Keeps for up to 1 week in the refrigerator or for up to 6 months in the freezer.

20 ripe tomatoes, stems and cores removed

2 large heads of garlic, divided into unpeeled cloves

½ cup extra-virgin olive oil

Kosher salt and freshly ground black pepper

8 sprigs fresh thyme

marinated chickpeas

3 cups dried chickpeas, or
4 cups drained canned
chickpeas

2 tablespoons plus 1 cup
extra-virgin olive oil

1 yellow onion, quartered

1 celery stalk, cut in half, plus
1 cup finely diced celery

2 medium carrots, peeled
and halved

4 sprigs fresh rosemary

2 sprigs fresh thyme

Kosher salt and freshly ground
black pepper

1 cup finely diced red onion

1 cup red wine vinegar

2 garlic cloves, crushed
and peeled

½ teaspoon chopped
peperoncini,
or ¼ teaspoon cayenne pepper

2 tablespoons chopped fresh
oregano, or 1 tablespoon dried
Sicilian oregano

1 cup finely chopped flat-leaf
parsley

Zest and juice from 1 lemon

MAKES 3 TO 4 CUPS

If using dried chickpeas, soak the chickpeas in water overnight and drain.

Heat 2 tablespoons of the oil in a large skillet over medium heat. Add the yellow onion, celery stalk, and carrots and cook, stirring occasionally, for about 15 minutes, until the vegetables begin to color. Tie 2 sprigs of rosemary and the thyme sprigs in cheesecloth and add to the vegetables. Add the chickpeas (soaked dried or canned) and enough water to cover by 2 inches. Bring to a gentle simmer and reduce the heat to medium-low. Season with salt and pepper, and cook for about 1½ hours, until the chickpeas are soft. Remove the skillet from the heat and set aside to cool completely. Drain, discarding vegetables and herbs.

In a bowl, combine the red onion and vinegar, and set aside for 15 minutes. Drain the onion and transfer to a large bowl. Add the diced celery, garlic, peperoncini, chickpeas, remaining 2 sprigs rosemary, oregano, parsley, remaining 1 cup oil, lemon zest, and lemon juice. Season with salt and pepper and mix well. Cover the bowl with plastic wrap and refrigerate for at least 1 hour, making sure to turn the mixture a couple of times while marinating. Allow the salad to come to room temperature before serving. Keeps well if refrigerated up to 3 to 4 days.

whole-grain mustard sauce

½ cup Dijon mustard

½ cup whole-grain mustard

⅓ cup ketchup

¼ cup drained Pickled Mustard
Seeds (page 187)

MAKES 1 TO 1½ CUPS

In a bowl, combine all the ingredients and mix well. Use immediately or store in the refrigerator for up to 2 weeks.

spinach-basil pesto

MAKES 1 TO 2 CUPS

Rinse the spinach leaves a few times until they have no sand left on them, and put them into a colander or strainer. Add the basil leaves and pour boiling water over them, making sure that they all get covered. Immediately submerge the spinach and basil in cold water. Once cool, squeeze the leaves to extract as much water as possible.

In a food processor, combine all the ingredients and process until it becomes a smooth paste. Season generously with salt and pepper. Use immediately or store in the refrigerator for up to 5 days.

1 cup packed spinach leaves

1 cup packed basil leaves

¼ cup grated Parmesan or Romano cheese

1 teaspoon chopped garlic

⅓ cup extra-virgin olive oil

2 tablespoons toasted pinenuts

Kosher salt and freshly ground black pepper

walnut pesto

MAKES ABOUT ¾ CUP

Preheat the oven to 300°F.

Distribute the walnuts on a sheet pan and toast in the oven until they are fragrant. Transfer the walnuts to a blender or food processor and roughly chop. Slowly add the oil and continue to process until you have a just spreadable but not too smooth pesto. (Keep in mind that the walnuts release their own oils, so be patient if the paste seems too dry at first.) Season with salt and pepper. Use immediately or store in the refrigerator for up to 1 week.

2 cups walnut pieces

¼ cup extra-virgin olive oil

Kosher salt and freshly ground black pepper

salsa verde

MAKES ABOUT 1½ CUPS

In a bowl, combine all the ingredients and mix well. Add the mixture to a food processor and process until they are well incorporated but not too smooth. Adjust the seasoning if necessary. The sauce should be tangy and salty. Keeps well refrigerated for up to 1 week.

5½ cups flat-leaf parsley leaves

2 tablespoons diced shallots

1 tablespoon chopped garlic

2 tablespoons drained capers

½ cup extra-virgin olive oil

2 tablespoons white wine vinegar

2 teaspoons kosher salt

1 teaspoon freshly ground black pepper

spiced walnuts

MAKES 1 CUP

Preheat the oven to 300°F.

In a bowl, combine the cumin, cinnamon, and nutmeg and mix in the honey. Add the walnuts and toss to coat. Sprinkle with the salt. Pour the nuts onto a sheet pan covered in waxed paper and toast in the oven, stirring frequently, for approximately 10 minutes, until they are dark golden in color. Allow to cool completely before using or storing in a dry place for up to 2 weeks.

¼ teaspoon ground cumin

¼ teaspoon ground cinnamon

¼ teaspoon grated nutmeg

1 tablespoon honey

1 cup walnuts halves

½ teaspoon kosher salt

lemon confit

12 lemons

5 shallots, peeled and minced

6 garlic cloves, minced

⅔ cup kosher salt

⅓ cup sugar

About 4 cups extra-virgin olive oil

MAKES ABOUT 4 CUPS

Plunge the lemons into a pot of boiling water (this softens any outer layer of wax). Drain, rinse, then wipe the lemons clean. Dry the lemons, then slice them very thin. Discard the ends and remove and discard the seeds. In a small bowl, combine the shallots with the garlic. In another bowl, mix the salt with the sugar.

Arrange a layer of lemon slices in the bottom of a medium container with a lid, making sure not to overlap the slices. Sprinkle the lemons first with a little shallot mixture, then with some salt and sugar mixture. Repeat, layering lemons in stacks and sprinkling them with the shallot and salt mixtures until the final lemon slices are topped with the last of the salt and shallot mixtures. As you carefully layer the lemons, layer in stacks. Cover the container and refrigerate for 3 days, flipping the stacks halfway through the process, allowing all the lemon to cure evenly.

Remove and drain the lemons in a strainer for 15 minutes or so. Discard the liquid. Pack the drained lemons tightly in a jar or other clean container and top off with oil, making sure to cover all the lemons. The confit can be used immediately or kept in the refrigerator for at least a month.

resources

Piccinini Brothers
633 Ninth Avenue
New York, NY 10036
www.piccininibros.com
Game, game birds, poultry, duck

D'Artagnan
Tel: 800-DARTAGN (800-327-8246), ext. 3
Fax: 973-465-1870
www.dartagnan.com
Artisan lamb, chicken, cured meats

Heritage Foods USA
www.heritagefoodsusa.com
Poultry, pork, beef, lamb, cured meats, pole-caught tuna, wild salmon, dry goods

Tallgrass Beef
www.tallgrassbeef.com
Grass-fed beef

Fra'Mani
www.framani.com
High-quality cured meats

Boccalone
www.boccalone.com
High-quality cured meats

Niman Ranch
www.nimanranch.com
Beef, lamb, pork

David's Old World Brand
www.deandeluca.com
Pastrami, ham, bacon

American Tuna
www.americantuna.com
Pole-caught tuna

Primizie Fine Foods
primiziefinefoods.myshopify.com
Pole-caught tuna, imported oils, spices, and preserves

Browne Trading Company
Tel: 800-944-7848
Fax: 207-766-2404
www.browne-trading.com
Fish, shellfish

Chefshop.com
www.chefshop.com
Imported oils, spices, preserves, olives

S.O.S. Chefs of New York
Tel: 212-508-5813
Fax: 212-505-5815
www.sos-chefs.com
atef@soschefs.com for e-mail orders
Spices, mushrooms, high-quality chocolate and cocoa powder, baking supplies

thanks

To the whole 'wichcraft team for your hard work and dedication, especially to Jeffrey, Jameson, Ben, Erica, and Amy, who joined the team very early on.

To Bob, Dick, and Jeanne for believing that making sandwiches was a good idea.

To Lori for the great name.

To Karen for providing such great dessert recipes and even making every one of them in our early days.

To everyone at Craft who helped us get started, especially Katie.

To Christina for an amazing job putting this book together; we really don't know if we would've ever made it without her.

To Damon and the entire Craft kitchen for assisting us during the testing and photography of this book.

To Rhona for translating the 'wichcraft story and philosophy to paper.

To Bill for capturing great images.

To all our bakers, farmers, and ranchers who, even though we know most of them by name, are too many to mention—for the great food you give us to work with.

To Noah at Fishs Eddy for providing us with the beautiful plates to showcase our food in this book.

To our regulars, who keep coming back for more and make us be proud of what we do.

To Sisha without whom there would be no 'wichcraft.

index

tuna and roasted tomato melt

fried eggs with bacon, gorgonzola, and frisée

onion frittata with roasted tomato and cheddar

gruy

cara

boucheron with grapefruit and crispy olives

oatmeal cream'

lobster with and tarragon

chocolate cream'wich

ana bread

h caramel

cream and

an brittle

roasted pumpkin with mozzarella and hazelnut brown butter

roasted squid po-boy with black chile oil

fontina with black trumpet mushrooms and truffle fondue

roasted

uschette

illet e 00

00

peanu

butte

cream

pbj

chopped chickpeas with roasted peppers, black olives, lemon confit, and parsley

raw yellow beets with avocado, grapefruit, and radish sprouts

fried squid po-boy and black chile oil

avocado opoova

marinated eggplant with chickpea puree, roasted peppers, and watercress

erbread with rum ice
n and poached pears

marinated

tuna with

beans, pic

peppers, g

and mayon

an-fried eggplant with buffalo mozzarella, white anchovies, and raisin-pinenut relish

smoked ham wit
avocado and bu

roasted asparagus w
onions, basil, and va

mquat-rosemary marmalade with

roast beef